PRAISE FOR *A HOOT IN HELL'S ISLAND*

"Most pilots fly the plane. The great ones put it on. . . . Hoot was a great stick."

—**Joe Mavretic**, Lieutenant Colonel, US Marine Corps, Retired, AKA "Leper," F8 (Crusader) and F4 (Phantom) Driver, Former Commanding Officer, Marine Fighter Attack Squadron 251: 1973–1975, and Former Speaker of the North Carolina House of Representatives

"If you want to be reminded of why America is known as 'the home of the brave,' then you need to read *A Hoot in Hell's Island*."

—**Santo J. Costa**, Retired Vice Chairman and President, Quintiles Transnational Corporation, Author of *Humanity at Work*

"Honestly, I could not put *A Hoot in Hell's Island* down, and I highly recommend it to anyone in a leadership position or who aspires to be in one. Colonel Kirk Warner has done a masterful job in capturing his uncle's attack pilot 'stories' and adding accurate, historical context. Although 'Hoot' called himself an 'average American,' there was nothing average about this Navy Cross recipient. Tom Brokaw called his generation the greatest, and I agree with him. 'Hoot' and his squadron mates personified the finest qualities of true warriors: vision, passion, total commitment, loyalty, heart, sense of humor, and courage, just to mention a few. Reading this book made me feel very fortunate to have had the opportunity to wear the same Navy 'Wings of Gold' as LCDR 'Hoot' Gibson, a true hero!"

—**Ralph E. "Benny" Suggs**, Rear Admiral, US Navy, Retired, Naval Aviator (attack aircraft A2, A6, A7, F14 Tomcat) and Former Commander, Carrier Group Six, Aircraft Carrier USS *America* (CV-66), and Attack Squadron VA-55

"Presented for the first time in full length, the wartime memoirs of decorated World War II dive bomber pilot Robert 'Hoot' Gibson are an enlightening look into an important era of American history. His nephew, Colonel Kirk Gibson Warner, has tastefully blended Hoot's full story from training through carrier combat with other historical segments to keep the action in perspective. Gibson was a true American hero, and Warner has done him great justice by sharing a rare snapshot of life under fire as documented by a man who survived one of the most challenging periods of the war, establishing himself as a flattop fighter of the first degree. No library of naval carrier aviation would be complete without this valuable narrative."

—**Stephen L. Moore**, Author of *Pacific Payback* and *The Battle for Hell's Island*

"In the era of industrial-scale warfare, conventional wisdom holds that single combatants exert little influence. But in the Pacific Theater of World War II, the individuals who determined battles and ultimately the fate of nations often were dive bomber pilots. Ranking high among them was Robert D. Gibson, who compiled an exceptional record in the carrier battles of 1942. Kirk Warner's tribute to his uncle is a valuable addition to the literature of the Pacific War."

—**Barrett Tillman,** Author of *On Wave and Wing: The 100-Year Quest to Perfect the Aircraft Carrier* and *Enterprise, America's Fightingest Ship and the Men Who Helped Win World War II*

"This gripping memoir describes Lt. Cmdr. Robert Gibson's life-or-death exploits as a top Navy dive bomber pilot at Midway and during the desperate struggle for Guadalcanal in 1942. It is both anecdotal and sweeping in scope. Navy Cross winner 'Hoot' Gibson clearly exemplified the very best of the America that won World War II."

—**Joseph Wheelan**, Author of *Midnight in the Pacific: Guadalcanal, the World War II Battle That Turned the Tide of War*

"This book chronicles the history of Navy Cross recipient Hoot Gibson during the critical early days of the Imperial Japanese Navy's World War II domination of the Pacific. Gibson's insights, in his own words, provide the reader with a front row seat to experience the development of the USN's operations against the Imperial Navy's onslaught. From the cockpit of his Dauntless dive bomber, he repeatedly braved the layers of the defenses thrown against him by Admiral Yamamoto's best. From the battle of Midway through the final naval battle of Guadalcanal, the future of the war hung in the balance. Without Gibson and men of his iron-willed determination, the world might have had a different fate."

—**Thomas C. Waskow**, Lieutenant General, US Air Force, Retired, O2-A (Skymaster) and F-15 (Eagle) Fighter Pilot, Former Commanding General, US Forces Japan, and Commander, 5th Air Force

"*A Hoot in Hell's Island* is a delightful read. Built on memoirs left by the author's uncle and adorned with historical context, the book brings to life fascinating and critical aspects of World War II in the Pacific, especially the Guadalcanal campaign. The book will flesh out knowledge of enthusiasts, and for those less informed, it provides the compelling inside story of an 'average American'—who performed heroic deeds when his nation needed selfless service. 'Hoot' Gibson . . . a great American!!"

—**Jack L. Rives**, Lieutenant General, US Air Force, Retired, Former Judge Advocate General of the Air Force

"A captivating read from two great Americans, 'Hoot' Gibson, a highly decorated Navy WW2 Dauntless pilot, and his nephew Col. Kirk Gibson Warner. Kirk brings Hoot's memoirs to life, from 'saddling up' on the Japanese heavy cruiser *Kinugasa* and scoring a direct hit to jinking and side-slipping to avoid certain death as a Japanese Zero Ace pilot runs out of bullets and finally pulls line abreast and salutes 'Hoot' for his superb airmanship. Two magnificent storytellers keep you turning the pages as we learn time-proven lessons of strength, courage, discipline, honor, camaraderie, and life.

—**William S. "Buz" Busby**, Major General, US Air Force, Retired, F-4 (Phantom) and F-16C (Fighting Falcon) Fighter Pilot, Former Commander, 149th Fighter Squadron and the 455th *Expeditionary* Operations Group, Bagram Air Base, Afghanistan

"Lt. Cmdr. Robert D. 'Hoot' Gibson provides a highly descriptive firsthand account as a naval aviator in the Pacific. *A Hoot in Hell's Island* is not your usual wartime memoir. Hoot served in the major naval campaigns in the Pacific War and recounts his experiences in a natural prose style with exceptional detail. Colonel Warner blends his uncle's narrative with clear and insightful historical notes, which seamlessly add to the flow and perspective of the accounts. This is a substantive work which will be invaluable to professional historians and to the public at large.

—**Joseph W. Caddell**, PhD, Teaching Associate Professor of History, University of North Carolina at Chapel Hill, and Adjunct Assistant Professor of History, North Carolina State University

"Kirk Warner and his uncle, Bob 'Hoot' Gibson, have created a WWII Navy pilot's version of the classic by E. B. Sledge, *With the Old Breed!* Using the language of the times, Hoot describes the harrowing and bitter fighting that our wounded and diminished Navy endured during the early part of the conflict from his front row seat in a Dauntless dive bomber. Often outnumbered and outgunned, our naval forces would return to the fight time and again, with little hope of surviving intact, and even more uncertain of victory. Often, our forces were given no relief or chance to recover. Carriers went into battle being repaired as they sailed! Their story redefines what is meant by NEVER QUIT. It is a remarkable and enjoyable read that reminds us why that generation of Americans truly exemplified the best of our citizen warriors."

—**David L. Hayden**, Colonel, US Army, Retired, Former Staff Judge Advocate of NORTHCOM, XVIII Airborne Corps, and 82nd Airborne Division

"A fantastic tale of air combat in World War II, told directly from the perspective of a tenacious and talented aviator. From incredible techniques of flight leadership, bombing, and strafing to humorous anecdotes of the Pacific War, Hoot's stories are a must-read for war historians and aviation enthusiasts alike. After reading *A Hoot in Hell's Island*, I wanted to jump back into the cockpit myself!"

—**Edward L. Jeep,** Colonel, US Marine Corps, Retired, Naval Aviator, CH-46E (Sea Knight) Pilot, and Former Commanding Officer, HMM-364 "Purple Foxes"

"This book is a riveting tale of WW II aviation combat by one of America's great combat aviation heroes. A humble man with incredible skills—and even greater luck in combat—tells his own story. This incredible and historic look at the air war in the Pacific is spellbinding in its raw realism and a man's quiet commitment to his country. At one time he writes, 'Our victory in the war was now my personal responsibility,' and his tale of death and destruction of the enemy in the air, on land, and at sea will give you goosebumps. 'No one can understand war who hasn't been to war,' but Navy Cross winner 'Hoot' Gibson does a unique job of lifting the veil."

—**Robert Adams**, MD, Colonel, US Army, Retired, Former Navy SEAL, and Author of *Six Days of Impossible: Navy SEAL Hell Week—A Doctor Looks Back*

"Hoot Gibson's story of the early days of the naval air campaign in the South Pacific as seen through the eyes of a Dauntless dive bomber pilot is gripping. From Midway through the harrowing campaign to secure Guadalcanal, we see World War II as a young Navy pilot, fresh from the hardscrabble of the hills of Missouri and flight training just before the war broke out, saw it. It renewed my appreciation for the remarkable efforts of young Americans who rallied to the country's cause as the war's outcome hung in the balance. Kirk Warner has done a top-notch job presenting his uncle's rich memoirs and providing deeper historical and operational context to Hoot's heroics. A remarkable story well told."

—**Charles B. Neely, Jr.,** Captain, US Navy, Retired, Former Combat Information Center Officer, USS *Regulus* (AF-57), Vietnam, 1965–1967

"A Hoot in Hell's Island is two books in one—a riveting account of the major battles in the Pacific Theater during World War II and a one-of-a-kind memoir from a carrier-based Navy pilot who was in the thick of the fighting and lived to tell about it. 'Hoot' Gibson's personal and unique account of the wartime environment, tragedies, and triumphs present a convincing reminder that victory and defeat in the Pacific Theater were still very much at stake in the autumn of 1942. We hear echoes from *Thirty Seconds Over Tokyo*, *Top Gun*, *Victory at Sea*, and *South Pacific*. Hoot's story provides both an exciting tale for the general reader and a valuable resource for the scholar.

> —**James R. Tootle**, PhD, Assistant Dean (Retired), College of Arts and Sciences, The Ohio State University

"Kirk Warner has lovingly shared his uncle's memories of training for and then executing the brutal reality of air war in the Pacific. 'Hoot' Gibson is an extraordinary example of an ordinary American boy tasked with that which is never ordinary."

> —**Bruce Brittain**, Author of *The Chow-Hound: The Ordinary Yet Extraordinary WWII Story of Courage, Sacrifice, Gratitude, Remembrance, Coincidence and Small Miracles*

"This captivating story describes a heroic Navy pilot flying dangerous combat missions in the Pacific during World War II. Colonel Warner narrates Hoot Gibson's action-packed wartime experiences. The reader can visualize the action as the pilot scouts for enemy ships, then dives his aircraft on perilous bombing runs and jinks his SBD bomber aircraft to avoid enemy fighters. It is truly amazing that he survived numerous close encounters with death. This is a great story filled with danger, humor, and intrigue. Readers will be convinced that the name of this brave pilot deserves a most prominent place in our nation's history."

> —**George W. Kohn**, Author of *Vector to Destiny: Journey of a Vietnam F-4 Fighter Pilot*

A Hoot In Hell's Island:
The Heroic Story of World War II Dive Bomber
Lt. Cmdr. Robert D. "Hoot" Gibson

by Col. Kirk Gibson Warner (USA, Ret.)
and Robert D. Gibson

ISBN 978-1-64663-642-6

Library of Congress Control Number: 2022902007

Published by

W WARNER BOOKS

kirkgwarner.com

A HOOT IN HELL'S ISLAND

THE HEROIC STORY OF WORLD WAR II DIVE BOMBER
LT. CMDR. ROBERT D. "HOOT" GIBSON

COL. KIRK GIBSON WARNER (USA, RET.)
AND ROBERT D. GIBSON

I wouldn't give a hoot in hell for a man who lost and laughed. That's why Americans have never lost, and will never, never lose a war; for the very thought of losing is hateful to an American.

—Lt. Gen. George S. Patton, US Third Army, 1944

This book is dedicated to my uncle, co-author, and hero Robert Douglas ("Hoot" or "Bob") Gibson (1919-2002), who in turn dedicated his memoirs to his father, my grandfather, Alexander Rowat Gibson and the hundreds of millions of other average Americans who built the greatest country in the world.

In thy faint slumbers I by thee have watch'd
And heard thee murmur tales of iron wars . . .

—William Shakespeare, *Henry IV*

If we are marked to die, we are enough
To do our country loss; and if to live,
The fewer men, the greater share of honor.

—William Shakespeare, *Henry V*

TABLE OF CONTENTS

· ❀ ·

AUTHOR'S NOTE

Robert D. "Hoot" Gibson's memories are told in a first person narrative.

Kirk Gibson Warner's commentary is presented in third person.

Additionally, each author's voice is visually represented typographically as demonstrated above.

SOUTH PACIFIC 1942

AMERICAN FORCES LAND and fight for control of Guadalcanal, a small but strategically pivotal island in the South Pacific. The Japanese want it back.

They call it *Jigoku no Shima*—Hell's Island.[1]

A bunch of tough Marines and a handful of pilots were not going to let them have it back. Their determination turned the tide in the Pacific.

Can the Americans hold?

"We'll stick."

—Admiral Ernest J. King, CIC, U.S. Fleet

---

1   Inspired and paraphrased from Stephen L. Moore, *The Battle for Hell's Island: How a Small Band of Carrier Dive-Bombers Helped Save Guadalcanal*, New York, NAL Caliber/Penguin Random, 2015.

INTRODUCTION

ROBERT DOUGLAS "HOOT" GIBSON was one of the Navy's most heralded Dauntless SBD dive-bomber pilots in the Pacific Theater in World War II. He earned a Navy Cross for his gallantry in battle in the Solomon Islands defending Guadalcanal in November 1942. He was part of the deadly Bombing Squadrons Five, Six, and Ten aboard the USS *Yorktown* and USS *Enterprise*. By War's end, Hoot had participated in three of the five carrier battles, as well as in the first invasion of the war, Guadalcanal, and its last, Borneo, which was his thirteenth battle.

Hoot had just returned to the *Yorktown* from a scout mission during the Battle of Midway when it was hit and foundered. He jumped off the *Yorktown,* was pulled from the oil-smothered sea, and survived several other water landings during the war. He gallantly served during the major South Pacific carrier campaigns, including all four famous battles in defense of Guadalcanal: Savo Island, Eastern Solomons, Santa Cruz, and the Naval Battle of Guadalcanal, and several infamous *Battles of the Royal Hawaiian Hotel*! He also flew with the Cactus Air Force at Henderson Field on Guadalcanal and was decorated by the Marines. He dropped the second bomb in the United States' first offensive at Guadalcanal—*Hell's Island.*

In those dark days of the Pacific War, the battle for Guadalcanal was still very much in doubt. Hoot sighted the Japanese Fleet heading for Guadalcanal. He proceeded to attack the vanguard ships, went into a steep dive, dropped his bomb right amidships, and destroyed the heavy cruiser *Kinugasa*. The magazines exploded and the great ship broke in half and sank.

Hoot also was credited with sinking two Japanese troop transports and an I-class submarine as well as shooting down two of the agile Zero fighters, going toe to toe with Japan's premier ace pilot. His actions alone eliminated thousands of Japanese troops from reinforcing enemy forces in the desperate struggle for Guadalcanal. His exploits filled the news media from coast to coast with headlines like: "Lt. Gibson is Navy's Sgt. York" and "Teacher gives Japs a Lesson in Subtraction."

But he was not just a heroic pilot. He was my uncle.

Uncle Bob was larger than life to me. He tried to capture and tell his remarkable journey in writing but died before he published it. I figure it is time to share his recollections and remarkable adventures, so I have tried to tell his story using his memoirs, battle narratives, news accounts, biographies, naval histories, and official US Navy records. I have reorganized, edited, sanded down, provided context, corroborated, and added some historiography to his wonderfully told tales of action in the Pacific War and in his life. But in the end, this is Hoot's story and memoirs. I trust it will *stick*, just like the Americans at Guadalcanal.

—COL. KIRK GIBSON WARNER (USA, RET.)

AVERAGE AMERICANS

Monument, Unionville Cemetery, Unionville, Missouri

LAST NIGHT AS I lay awake, I thought about my father, A.R. Gibson, who married and raised his family in a rural town in the northern hills of Missouri. He was a stonecutter, as were his father and grandfather before him in Scotland. A.R. was conceived in the 1880s in Scotland before his parents emigrated to Des Moines, Iowa, to help build the state Capitol building in stone. Therefore, I have always bragged that my dad came from Scotland. My father also told us that we had 300 cousins in Kilmarnock, Scotland. On a recent visit to that small city, I found 1,000 Gibsons listed in the phone book.

When A.R. reached twenty-five, he bought a monument works in Unionville, Missouri, and eventually had four sales offices in other small towns. The countryside was hilly and thus was not valuable for farming, so the sparse population had to really scratch for a living. My siblings and I were dedicated to getting out of that setting as soon as possible. For the most part, we did just that. I speeded up my high school days to finish in three years in order to look for a life of more opportunity.

Looking back, the town taught me many more desirable lessons that really outweighed the dreary aspects associated with nonachievement. But the real point of this message is to say that my dad erected the largest monument in the country cemetery, upon which was inscribed:

THE GIBSONS
AVERAGE AMERICANS

· 🍀 ·

The Gibsons were anything but. They were the exceptional arising from the ordinary. One such rarity was my Uncle Hoot.

It follows then as certain as that night succeeds the day, that without a decisive Naval force we can do nothing definitive. And with it, every thing honourable and glorious. A constant Naval superiority would terminate the War speedily; without it, I do not know that it will ever be terminated honourably.

—Gen. George Washington to Marquis de LaFayette,
November 15, 1781

CHAPTER ONE

UNIONVILLE

Pop, Alexander Rowat Gibson

IT WAS 1933. My father, the sheriff, handed each of us a shotgun. I was thirteen years old. He said, "Pretty Boy Floyd was seen in those woods. We are going to get him. He's armed and dangerous, so shoot to kill." I took my position in the manhunt as we spread through the forest. I was supremely confident that I could kill Floyd before he could kill me. I was wondering, too, how many flying squirrels Floyd had killed on the wing with a rifle.

· ✿ ·

FLYBOYS

My early recollections of aviation are from Unionville, Missouri. Probably my first was the day a barnstormer came to town with a biplane. My father took me and one of my brothers out to the cow pasture where the plane had landed and the three of us got in the rear open cockpit. He held one of us on each knee, and the plane took off from the field, circled the town, and came back to land. It was probably a ten-minute flight.

Another recollection was when I was eight and we drove by Lindbergh's birthplace in Saint Cloud, Minnesota. That was right after his first transatlantic flight in 1927.

I recall hearing stories about Jessie and Georgie Crockett, barnstormers from Unionville. Jessie was killed in a plane crash in a cow pasture. Everyone remarked what a dangerous and hazardous occupation that barnstorming was. Georgie went on to become a successful pioneer in aviation. He started an airline and air terminal in Las Vegas and later sold the airline to Howard Hughes. The airline was appropriately called Alamo Airways for Georgie Crockett, a descendant of Davy Crockett.

In the early pioneer days there was a man named Eddie Brice from Unionville who was also a barnstormer. He went to Central America to fly mail, passengers, chickens, and other cargo in old-fashioned planes. The natives learned to travel by airplane as the roads were non-existent. They'd get on with their turkeys or chickens or pigs and fly into Honduras, Guatemala, and Nicaragua to sell their products.

My next introduction to aviation was one day when I was in school at the University of Missouri. I was in St. Louis visiting a friend who was going to school at Washington University. We went to his fraternity where two of his fraternity brothers said, "Oh, we're going to go out and fly an airplane this afternoon." My reaction was that they were damn fools.

But, I guess my father was one of them. And I would follow his lead.

· ❦ ·

DEAD RECKONING

My father, Alexander Rowat "A.R." Gibson, bought a Luscombe airplane in Kansas City. It was an all-metal two-seater with fixed landing gear. He probably had ten hours of instruction on flying at best. He was fifty-eight years old. Pop would fly along the highway, and then occasionally he'd fly up into the clouds and get turned around. He'd usually end up in the opposite direction from where he was intending to go. One time he was flying from Kansas City back to Unionville and got lost in the clouds. Instead of going east, he finally came through the clouds and landed in a cornfield where he nosed it over. He was about 200 miles west of Kansas City, instead of east of it. He didn't pay too much attention to the compass and other niceties of safe flying. Those were just minor things to worry about to my father. He had supreme confidence that he could handle any situation and thrived on excitement. He was, after all, a big frog in a small pond.

On one trip he and his passenger had flown to Miami, where one of them said, "Let's go to Havana and do some gambling." So, they flew to Havana, Cuba just by dead reckoning. They next decided to fly to Mexico City. On their way to Mexico City, A.R. found that he was lost, but he saw men down below. He sat the plane down on a dusty road. There were maybe thirty or forty Mexican peons with their machetes working in the fields, and A.R. and his passenger were a little apprehensive. They thought, "What have we gotten into here? They'll just cut our heads off." It seemed a trivial problem that they didn't speak Spanish. Well, he just waved his arms and said "Mexico City?" and kept pointing in different directions. And they said, "Oh, si, Señor, Mexico City is this way." So A.R. got in the plane and took off. Eventually, he found Mexico City and they spent several days there and then flew home.

Being conceived in Scotland, Pop was an avid golfer. He founded the Unionville Country Club with its nine holes and sand greens, which required each golfer to drag a path for putting his ball. Dragging a path in the sand was about two feet wide, and you could still miss a putt by a considerable amount. So it didn't ensure that you were going to sink the putt. All it did was make a smooth surface to avoid running over a bunch of twigs.

One of the reasons he bought a plane was to travel to other country clubs to play golf. When the Unionville Country Club was closed, he flew to Ottumwa, Iowa and took me with him. He had friends up there playing. We were going up to watch them. We flew in and landed on the fairway, then taxied up to the green where they were putting. After much to-do with the golfers, A.R. decided to take off downhill from the green, which also happened to be downwind. Downwind take offs are a serious no-no in flying.

A row of big, tall maple trees grew at the end of the fairway, down by the tee box. We couldn't get up enough air speed going down wind, but finally got a few feet off the ground. A.R. kept pulling back the stick to try to get over these tall trees, but the plane mushed in. There were a bunch of little sapling trees along the side of the fairway, and we started clipping those with our wing, so that the plane spun around. Here we were with a damaged plane, sitting on the fairway at the country club, but at least we hadn't augured in. Messing around with the basics of flight usually means death. But our attempt was much to the amusement of all the players who were out there.

Of course, the Civil Aeronautics Authority came out and raised hell about it because it was against the law, even in those days. If this had happened at the Unionville Country Club, no one would have ever known about it. Realize that Unionville and the countryside around it was really another country in itself. It was self-sufficient and the Feds could be run out of town. My dad never drank. I only ever saw him take more than one or two drinks in his life. After the crash on the golf course, we went in and had dinner. He did have a drink that night.

One of the first planes he owned was a J-3 Piper Cub. The skin was made of canvas and painted bright yellow. The first ones had a thirty-horsepower engine. It was a little putt-putt, and if there was a very strong wind, you sort of found yourself going backward. Going down the highway, you wouldn't make much progress.

This is the plane in which A.R. landed on the cow pasture. Just as his wheels hit the ground, a cow walked right in front of him, so he hit the throttle and nosed it down to hit the wheels on the ground, pulled the stick back, and just bounced over the cow. When he got on the other side of the cow, the plane nosed over. He was in the back seat, because the seats were tandem, with one seat in front of the other. The back of the seat in front had an iron bar that went up and curved around. As he nosed over, his mouth hit the bar of the seat in front and knocked out several of his teeth. Before he would leave the plane, he fumbled down on the bottom of the floor to find his gold teeth that had been knocked out, putting them in his pocket to reuse when he went to the doctor.

Come to think about it, A.R. was one of the early pioneers in aviation. Aviation was not really very advanced, even at the airlines. Unless you were a fighter ace like Eddie Rickenbacker, most pilots never really had any formal training in that era. Aviation was just starting a formalized sort of training program.

A.R. "Pop" Gibson, on his Navion Airplane

CHARACTERS

You could drive to within forty miles of Unionville, and the rest of the way you had to swing in on trees, or at least that was how it seemed. It was still a bit of the Old West and my pop was the sheriff. When folks were killed, Pop would investigate and lock the shooter up if it was murder. He ran the monument works, so he also cashed in by selling the family of the victim a tombstone.

Merle Mulinex was murdered in cold blood by Bugs Mills. He was acquitted though, since Merle was caught in bed with Bugs' wife. That woman was a doozy. As sheriff, my dad raided her house, as she was a known bootlegger and these were Prohibition years. As he burst in the door, he saw her throw a bottle out the kitchen window. As A.R. leaned out the window to look in the darkness for the hooch, she just grabbed his feet, and tossed him out, right on his head. He came running back around the house, and coldcocked her—hit her right on the chin and knocked her out cold. A.R. was a semi-professional boxer when he was young so knew how to throw a hard punch. Then A.R. grabbed her by her feet, dragged her into the car, and threw her in jail.

Thinking about the old jailhouse, my brother Jim always said a prisoner could blow the walls down by sneezing. One day, A.R. got wind that a prisoner planned a jail break that night. He crept up nearby and laid waiting in a ditch. As the man emerged from a hole in the jailhouse wall, A.R. stood up and yelled, "Stop or I'll shoot." The man did not stop and A.R. did shoot. The man was taken to the top floor of the courthouse and put into a cell where A.R. held prisoners for testifying at their trials in the adjoining courtroom. The Gibson boys followed the doctor upstairs to watch him as he dug out the No. 1 buckshot from the prisoner's rear end.

We were most impressed with the security of that cell inside the courthouse until one Saturday night at the very height of the town square walk-arounds, our minds were boggled as we stood in front of Lathrop's Drug Store. A prisoner was lowering himself by sheets tied together right down to the courthouse lawn. My friends and I yelled in glee!

A few times I rode in the car with A.R. when he was taking a prisoner to the state prison. I certainly found out what life is like in a prison. That would have been good therapy for anyone planning to get into trouble. They would find out the penalty was too great. On occasion A.R. would make friends with a white-collar prisoner during a lengthy trial. Then A.R. would bring the prisoner home to stay at our house the night before in order to get an early start to prison in Jefferson City in the morning.

One Sunday, my dad was taking us to a matinee at the Royal Theater in Unionville, and saw Arthur Weber, who was a bootlegger, talking to someone in a car. A.R. went over and grabbed his arm because he knew Arthur was selling this man alcohol. Arthur crashed the bottle onto the pavement to get rid of the evidence. A.R. told me to go get a coke bottle and he got his handkerchief out to soak up the alcohol. Meanwhile, Weber took off up the courthouse lawn and the town marshal Charlie Ackley happened to be there and took out his revolver and pointed it at Weber. His hand was shaking so much from fear that I was ready to dive under the car for safety. Weber made a run for it. My dad had soaked up and safeguarded the alcohol, so we all started off on the run to catch Weber. He hid in the loft of a grain mill. Later that evening he snuck over to his attorney Clare McGee's house. The next day Weber went to court and the judge ruled that A.R. couldn't admit the alcohol as evidence.

Weber's lawyer Clare McGee had several cousins from the eastern part of Putnam County, a town called Lickskillet, where the men were real drinkers and had hot tempers. Clare could hold his own in hot tempers as well. One cousin was a doctor in Unionville who was attacked in his clinic by a third cousin who opened up the doctor's gut with a knife. Clare heard about that and grabbed a gun and ran over to the east side of the square to encounter the third cousin. Clare fired two shots. One hit Hershell Pinson in the leg as he sat in front of Yount's Restaurant on a bench. The second shot hit the third cousin between the eyes.

Clare was let off because he had fired in a fit of passion, and then he was elected United States Congressman from our district. After the war he called me to Washington and asked me to enter politics and run for any state or national office because of my war record. I relied on A.R. for advice and he said, "Don't do it. Politics are dirty." I declined Clare's offer.

You couldn't avoid a town character in Unionville. They were too obvious and too many. In fact, everyone in Unionville was a character. Hey, we were *all* characters! One was a fellow who ran for sheriff but was defeated so badly that the next day he came downtown wearing two six-shooters, one on each hip. He said he figured anyone that would get as few votes as he did needed to protect himself. Our town marshal was redheaded, and he had a big red moustache. He dressed exactly as Wyatt Earp did in Tombstone. His uniform included a black ten-gallon hat. He wore a black vest, white shirt, black pants, and a black tie.

My dad was in the cemetery one day chiseling numbers on a monument and had put his straw hat on another monument. All of a sudden, he looked around and the hat was gone. He saw Halley Mills running off with his hat stuck under her skirt. Halley lived by scavenging around in garbage cans. One time she moved into an abandoned house. Another time she was chased out from living under someone else's house. Halley was just another example of ordinary life in Unionville.

Ed Christi ran the hotel in Unionville—The Staples Hotel. One morning a customer complained to Ed that there had been a rat fight in his room the night before. Ed replied, "What the hell do you expect for two dollars, a bull fight?"

EDUCATION

My father took me hunting from the time I was ten years old. At that age I was given a shotgun and a rifle and became an expert in shooting quail in flight with that shotgun. Occasionally, I could hit a flying squirrel, on the wing, with a rifle. Certain squirrels have flabby skin connecting their four legs and their bodies. When all four legs were spread-eagled, the skin was stretched out to simulate a parasail. Thus, they could fly from one tree to another. This lesson of leading the shot to the anticipated location of the squirrel was an invaluable one in my life.

· 🍁 ·

MIGHTY MIDGETS!

Perhaps fitting to its many humble characters, Unionville High School was the home of the *Midgets*. The best story on the origin of their moniker is that the circus came through town in the early 1900s and a couple of midgets got drunk and beat up the town bully. The high school football coach told his team that if they fought as hard as those midgets, they couldn't lose. And it stuck. They are now the Putnam County Midgets. The Mighty Midgets are, of course, in the Missouri small school division.

· 🍁 ·

In high school at Unionville, the summer after my sophomore year, I played in a band concert and afterward, my brother Roger, Stewart "Tudie" Pratt, and I drove to a little town nearby called Livonia that was having a county fair. We were driving at night, and all of a sudden, I woke up and was in bed and it was the next day.

I learned we'd been in a wreck. A fellow was drunk and driving a truck coming up the road on the wrong side without any lights on, and we ran smack into him. Killed him instantly, and then we were all thrown out of the car. The car's taillights didn't go off, so some jerk came along and twisted the key to turn it off and the car caught on fire and burned up.

Meanwhile, I was lying in a ditch with a concussion. While I was recuperating in bed, the superintendent of schools came out to see me and I asked for permission to graduate after my junior year. I had enough credits, as I had been carrying extra courses. He said it was okay, and it happened.

Upon graduation, I received a scholarship to go to Kirksville State Teacher's College. My brother Rankin had gone there one year before going to Missouri University at Columbia to law school. So, I did the same and transferred to Columbia the next year, because it was a much better school.

During my first year of college, four of us from Unionville roomed together in one house, and we had a good time. Then I joined a fraternity and we moved to another house and raised more hell. I guess we got kicked out of the first house. That first year of college we had an early spring, and it was really beautiful, with flowers and blossoms that were great and a lot of pretty girls. I found some good friends at the fraternity, and we'd go out to drink beer all night and raise hell and date girls. So, my academics were not stellar that spring. Even so, my previous reputation carried me through, and I still carried a B average. Attending the University of Missouri was a different story, as I found music to be my cup of tea, so I finished the last three years in college on the Dean's List.

The university was in the town of Columbia. As students, my brother Rankin and I worked for an apartment house between campus and the football stadium. For every home game we supplied our friends with a party. We furnished all mixers, and the attendees brought their own booze. We had all sorts of people coming in and out of the apartment. Even friends of friends showed up. People were always leaving their coats, so routinely on each following Monday, we would take the forsaken clothing and sell all of it at a pawnshop.

There was a bell tower next to the Geology building. One night, someone took a cow up in the bell tower, and the school had considerable trouble getting the cow back down. We watched with some glee.

When I graduated from college in June of 1940, I signed a contract to teach school near St. Louis, Missouri, in the southern suburban district called LeMay Ferry, on the west bank of the Mississippi River.

My classroom was on the ground floor and my desk faced east. As I looked out of the windows, I could see airplanes across the Mississippi River flying from Parks Air College. I got to think about this all day long, as I disliked teaching. As I was sitting in the classroom, I became curious about aviation.

CHAPTER TWO

WINGS

*"I was scheduled to qualify for carrier landings
on the Saratoga on Sunday, December 7."*

Hoot Gibson (right) with Hal Buell (center) and Hank Hartman in front
of a Navy SBC-4, Lambert Field, Naval Reserve Air Station, Robertson,
Missouri, January 1941

IN *THE BATTLE for Hell's Island*, historian Stephen Moore introduces us to pre-war Navy pilot training . . . and to Hoot:

Thousands of young men aspired to become naval aviators in the early 1940s. The process consumed the better part of a year, during which the aviation cadets faced injury, death, or washout nearly every day. The prize for possessing "the stuff" to make it through the program was being pinned with golden wings and being commissioned as an ensign in the US Navy. Bob Gibson met several other cadet pilots at their elimination base ("E-base") training. They were destined to see more of each other during 1942.

Robert Douglas Gibson was from Unionville, Missouri. He also had the advantage of having taken a college flight training program in a Piper Cub. Bob had graduated from college in June 1940 but found that his job as a high school music teacher was not satisfying. Bob and another teacher signed up for pilot CPT (civilian pilot training) and began taking lessons.

"Learning to fly was a snap," Bob said. At the end of his training program, he and three flying school buddies decided to seek further adventures by joining a military service in which they could really develop their flight careers. They picked the Navy, with twenty-year-old Bob obtaining his father's permission to sign up. His teaching career would have to wait.

Bob was the son of a sheriff who had taught him to become an excellent marksman from the age of ten. His nickname during flight schools quickly became "Hoot," in reference to the American rodeo champion and pioneer cowboy film actor Edmund "Hoot" Gibson. Hoot, one of the largest box-office draws in western films, appeared in his own books and even flew airplanes, so Bob Gibson's nickname just seemed to fit.

Hoot Gibson met twenty-nine other potential aviators at the St. Louis E-base training. His first instructor was a former dive-bomber pilot named Bruce Weber. "Bruce let me know in short order that I knew 'zilch' about flying," said Gibson. "And I was smart enough to answer, 'Aye, aye, sir!'" His CPT training was more than enough to get him through E-base and on to his next training assignment in Jacksonville, Florida. Hoot and three E-base buddies—Bill Branham, Mark Boyer, and Dave Chafee—piled into Gibson's car and set out for Florida. Gibson was particularly close with Chafee, a wavy, red-haired graduate of Baldwin-Wallace University in Ohio. Dave's good looks, cheerful personality, and strong singing voice helped charm the ladies wherever the quartet roamed in the ensuing months.[2]

· ❧ ·

IN THE NAVY

I didn't really like teaching music, so I took a civilian pilot training program in my free time. By the time I got through the training program in a Piper Cub, five of us decided to join the military to really learn how to fly. The superintendent of schools where I had been teaching was a German, and he raised hell when I resigned. He said, "I'll see that you never get another job. I'll blackball you." It's true that I had broken my contract. When I told the Navy, they said they'd take care of it, and I never heard another word from the superintendent.

The five of us, bravely calling ourselves the *Fighting Five*, loaded into my car with the mission to take a look at all opportunities. The first source we investigated was the Navy. When we burst into the Navy office at Lambert Field in St. Louis, a wise old Navy chief said, "Look,

---

2   Reprinted with permission. Stephen L. Moore, *The Battle for Hell's Island: How a Small Band of Carrier Dive-Bombers Helped Save Guadalcanal*, New York: NAL Caliber/ Penguin Random. 2015, 65-68 (hereafter "Hell's Island").

you birds, if you think you have what it takes here's your chance. Go topside and see if you can pass the physical examination." So, up the ladder we went and took our exams. Upon returning to the chief, he said, "Boys, you are now in the Navy."

We yelled and joined the Navy on the spot. Fortunately. If we had joined the Army, we would more likely have been killed. The Army was rapidly expanding, giving a lesser degree of training, and paying the price in much higher training and operating deaths. The Navy, meanwhile, adhered to tradition and gave a full measure of paternal supervision to its fledgling aviators.

Bill Branham was the best looking of the Fighting Five, so we assigned him as the bird dog to flush out good-looking girls. Bill always had a bevy of good-lookers around him, and I always made sure that I was there to give him a helping hand. When we made it to Pearl Harbor, we found that the ratio in Honolulu was about one girl for each 20,000 boys. A wonderful ratio for the girls, but most boys were at a gross handicap. Except for me because I had my private secret weapon, Bill Branham.

In repayment later in the war, and in the South Pacific where there were no girls, I met up with Bill and treated him on the *Enterprise* to a hot shower, a dinner on a linen cloth with silver napkin rings and waiters, and I followed up with a Betty Grable movie. Bill felt I had repaid my debt in full.

We had a lot of fun training in St. Louis. We went to what they called an *elimination base* where we flew eight hours in an N3N, the Navy's equivalent of the Boeing-Stearman N2S. When we completed the hours, the five of us hopped into my car and headed to Pensacola. We ended up moving to a new Naval Air Station at Jacksonville first. The schedule included getting up every morning and doing calisthenics at five o'clock while we froze our asses off, and then we'd march. I suppose marching is good for making officers out of a crummy bunch of civilians. One day, Franklin D. Roosevelt came down to review the station, so we stood at attention. I was in the front row when he drove by. That was the first time I had seen a president, but I haven't seen many since.

Then we were transferred to Pensacola. Again, the same five drove there in my car. En-route we took a lay-over at Tallahassee, where we had discovered a girls' school. Later, that school became part of Florida State University.

In those days there were four squadrons in the training syllabus. Squadron One was basic training. We learned the inside deal. If you could get through basic training in the N3Ns or N2S Stearman you would have proven you could fly. In Squadron Two, we flew old, retired service aircraft. They said if you didn't get killed in Squadron Two, you proceeded to the third squadron—instrument training. If you didn't go crazy in Squadron Three, you were on the road to getting a commission as an ensign in the Navy. At the end of Squadron Three, the Navy divided the cadets. The ones who went into carrier training were transferred to Opa Locka Naval Air Station near Miami, the others went to multi-engine seaplanes and stayed in Pensacola.

• ❀ •

"Two of Bob's flight training buddies were Dave Chafee and Steve Czarnecki. They were struggling with make the proper tail-first landing approach necessary for future flight operations. Bob was easily passing muster in Squadron One and 'spent many hours giving both Dave and Steve encouragement to conquer their devils of flight.' This would later give Hoot pause after both Chafee and Czarnecki died in tough situations in the Pacific."[3]

• ❀ •

OPA LOCKA

I finished Squadron Three in March 1941. Some of my friends stayed in Pensacola and went to training in flying *P boats*, multi-engine patrol

3   Moore, *Hell's Island*, 68.

planes, or float-planes off of cruisers. I was sent to Opa Locka. At the air station there, we flew more recently retired service planes from the Fleet.

In Squadron Two the planes were really old clunkers built right after World War I. They were all biplanes that required cranking the flaps up and down. Some had fixed landing gear, and some had landing gear you cranked up. I flew seven or eight different aircraft models: Chance-Vought, Vought, Boeing, and Curtiss. When we got to Opa Locka the more recently retired planes were basically still biplanes, like the F2Fs, F3Fs, and the Curtis-Wright biplanes. We got into some monoplanes, such as the Brewster F2A "Buffalo," the "Helldiver," and the BT built by Northrup as the forerunner of the SBD (Scout Bomber Douglas also known as the "Dauntless"), only with a much smaller engine at 550 hp. We did a lot of formation flying, gunnery, dive-bombing, and acrobatics. We had done acrobatics in Squadron One and we continued this at Opa Locka. The instructor would check pilots out while sitting on a chair in the shade of the hangar and watch us fly over the hangar. We did a certain routine just like the acrobatic teams do now, only individually, and it was fun.

Florida had huge, beautiful cumulus clouds to fly in and out of and through while chasing tails with other planes. There was also training in gunnery and dive-bombing. Those dive-bombers required coming over the target to be visible through a glass window in the bottom of the plane between the rudder pedals. When the target appeared in the window it was a signal to roll over and dive on it. The problem with such a procedure came from engine oil that leaked on the belly of the plane, including the window. It was very elementary, but not too reliable.

In the previous squadrons we became totally at ease flying with hundreds of other airplanes in the same air, protected by strict procedures. However, being one of several hundred planes circling a field at night became a little hairier at Opa Locka, mainly because of the age of the hotter (faster) planes we were now flying. Age affected the lighting systems in the planes, and one never knew when his lights would go off. Age also caused the connecting tubes to leak, and the smell of oil on hot pistons was always present.

Usually, night flights were scheduled in two sections. Our preference was to get the first flight, survive it, and then head for a funky bar just outside the main gate. With cold beers in hand, we would laugh at the poor suckers now in the air milling around overhead.

· ❁ ·

One night we experienced a hurricane that the Navy had prepared for by putting wooden slats over all the windows in our barracks. Later in the war, I experienced two hurricanes in Corpus Christi, Texas, but escaped them as we pilots flew all the planes inland to Del Rio, Texas. When I was a child, I had listened on a crystal-set radio to Dr. Brinkley's radio station in Del Rio. His specialty was grafting goat glands onto humans to improve their sex experiences. He was gone by the time I got to Del Rio, damn it!

· ❁ ·

DIVE-BOMBING 101

"Dive bombing an enemy ship that was twisting and turning at twenty-five to thirty knots was "similar to dropping a marble from eye height on a scampering cockroach."[4]

What the hell is dive-bombing and why were we training to do it? The British carrier groups had actually originated the concept of dive-bombing. We know that in World War II, though, the Brits gave up dive-bombing and relied instead on torpedoes. British and Japanese torpedoes were light years ahead of ours. As a result, America was even more dependent upon dive bombing to tame the Japanese hordes. Only two nations used dive-bombing in naval battles during WWII, the Japanese and the Americans.

---

4   Quotation from Lt. Cmdr. Maxwell F. Leslie, Commander, VB-3, USS *Yorktown* cited in Craig L. Symonds, *The Battle of Midway*. New York: Oxford University Press, 2011, 53.

Even so, dive-bombing proved to be the most effective bombing method for hitting moving ships. High-altitude horizontal bombing just doesn't cut the mustard. I had figured out that by the time a bomb drops from 20,000 feet, a ship at 30 knots can move within a half-mile square box in any direction. That's the reason horizontal bombing didn't work. As good as dive-bombing was, it lacked a lot, too. The results of any dive depended upon the skill and determination of each pilot.

The dive-bombing training method used involved dropping two-and-a-half pound practice bombs—little aluminum bombs that had a shotgun shell inside to explode when it hit the earth's surface, making contact visible with a puff of smoke. The practice bomb's trajectory also had its flaws, one of which included tumbling and influence by the drift of the plane and the winds.

I doubt if anyone in the Navy had dropped many live bombs until after the war started. The first live bomb most pilots dropped was on a Japanese target. A 500- or 1,000-pound bomb travels differently from a two-and-a-half-pounder that tumbles. The large bombs nearly continue the trajectory that the plane is taking at the time of release. Instructors taught us to figure out the surface wind velocity and direction, but that means little when diving from a high altitude. There was no way to tell what you were coming through because of the many different layers of wind changes, so who ever knew? That was pretty frustrating.

But soon I found out a way to hit and never miss. I always stuck on the ship and rode it as if in a saddle on the turning ship. If you're going in the same direction the ship is going, stick on its back, corkscrew with it as it turns, and make your release low enough—it hits every time! I had four hits and four drops on moving targets.

I've known Ed Heineman, the engineer who designed the SBD, a marvelous, first and maybe only plane that could reach *zero lift* on the wings. That meant that the airplane was diving on a collision course with a moving ship, so the bomb, when released, would continue traveling on a collision course. Releasing at 300 miles per hour, a bomb collides with the moving target in less than four seconds. Done properly, there was no escape for the target. By keeping the airplane in smooth vertical flight, no skidding, the rifle-shot-like bomb automatically compensates for the tight turns of the ship. Keeping the bombsight pipper on the smokestack could put the bomb right down the stack.

Also, you must dive at an angle beyond 90 degrees to ensure doing a 90-degree dive. Diving in a 90-degree attitude was actually in a 70-degree dive because the plane still had forward lift on the wings. You could still corkscrew. If you got on top of a ship and aimed for the smokestack, and kept the pipper on it, you could get ready for a hit.

· ✽ ·

NORTH ISLAND

The first of September 1941, I graduated from Opa Locka. The Navy gave me wings with a commission as an ensign. My assignment was to Bombing Squadron 2 on the USS *Lexington*. The program was that we would get further training at North Island, San Diego, California, in the Advanced Carrier Training Unit (ACTU). We were then into flying the actual service planes (SBDs) that we would fly overseas.

Ensign Robert D. Gibson, September 1941

Thirty of us arrived at North Island Naval Air Station from Pensacola with maybe some fellas from Jacksonville. A third base they were opening up was at Corpus Christi about that time in September 1941. Every night was our last night in port, you know, so we had to raise hell every night. We practiced bombing where Miramar Air Base is today but was then known as Fort Kearney. Circular targets were etched on the mesa tops for our practice flights out of North Island.

Upon arriving at North Island, the

Navy put us in Bachelor Officer Quarters, which we thought were just magnificent, with beautiful Spanish-style buildings, abundant and lush flowers, and green grass. In the Bachelor Officer Quarters we had a junior officer mess. You paid $10 for a share and then made profits on the drinks. When the value of your share got up to $20, they'd give you $10 back. They'd let you buy up to four shares and I always bought four shares and made sure that the value went up, as any good stockholder should do.

The most popular drinks for our crowd then were *stengahs* and *French 75s* made with champagne and cognac. Elated, we thirty pilots loved every minute of each day. We thought we were in the big leagues. All pilots in the group were single. The Navy required new pilots to be single for one year after graduation. Later the Navy relaxed that. Once you got your wings, you could get married. Some fellows got married on the q.t., but not many.

We bombed at Kearney, and at Otay Mesa, near Tijuana, where the Navy built a landing strip. Our landing area on North Island was simply a big mat. It didn't have runways, just a huge, paved surface that permitted a plane to land right into the wind.

· ❉ ·

FILMING WITH DISNEY

The strip on Otay Mesa was chosen for the filming of a training movie for pilots learning to land on a carrier. Walt Disney himself was hired to make the movie, and I was one of the pilots in the cast. We had a meeting with Disney at North Island to discuss the plans laid out for him by the Navy. We then loaded Disney and his equipment and a landing signal officer into the planes and flew to Otay, where we pilots shot simulated carrier landings. There were no restraining wires to stop the plane, however, just markings within which the plane must touch down. Many of my landings were filmed by Walt himself.

Upon returning to North Island, I told Disney, "You and I had the same piano teacher. Do you remember Maude Whitmore?"

Disney replied, "I certainly do!"

Then I elaborated, "She became my teacher, too, and she prominently displayed a drawing in color that you had made and given her when you were a child taking lessons on the piano. Am I right?"

Disney smiled and said, "Everything you have said is true."

· ✤ ·

SLOW BUT DEADLY

The approach all planes followed in preparing to land at North Island required flying up the Silver Strand—a strip of beach running northerly starting near Mexico and connecting to North Island. The flight approach included flying over the Hotel del Coronado that inspired each pilot with views of the lovely ladies sunning at the hotel and beach. At the end of the day, we'd step across the street to the BOQ bar, have a couple drinks, then head out to the Hotel del Coronado to have a few more drinks and another fly-by with the lovely ladies.

It seemed like I was one of the only guys with a car. When there was a traffic ticket, I was the designee. One night, late, I loaded the car with friends to drive to our quarters from the hotel on Orange Street, a two-way street with a divider. Unfortunately, I was driving down the wrong side and met a car head on. It was a police car! The police said, "You boys get on home and go to bed." They were very kind to the Navy.

We often did formation and night flying, but for the most part, every day we did dive bombing. On each flight we'd do five dives. The airplane we were training in was to be the one we would fly in combat— the SBD, which we called the *Slow But Deadly*. The SBD could hardly maintain a climb rate of 500 feet a minute, at least at lower altitudes. It took a while to climb up to 10,000 or 20,000 feet. By the time the pilot had done that five times, it was a long flight. Then it was time to return to the base.

At San Diego and overseas, we would often average five target-practice dives a day. I've probably made a thousand dives. The idea was that a flier had to do it in his sleep. By the time I was stationed on a carrier, I had more than 400 hours of flight time, which enabled me to function effectively. A lot of my friends who went into the Army and into combat had only a couple hundred hours. However, the next 200 are vital for survival. Four hundred hours in a plane were necessary to really get to know the plane. I'd say that if had I joined the Army, I'd have been killed for sure. I came close to it in the Navy. Within the next year I had 900 hours in the SBD. With significant time, pilots learn the important things that can save their lives. There are no shortcuts to experience.

· ❁ ·

DECEMBER 7, 1941

I had dinner with my half-sister Elsie and her husband at the North Island Officer's Club on Saturday night, December 6. We went to the San Diego Zoo the next day and while we were there, they announced the Pearl Harbor attack over the broadcast system and ordered all servicemen to return to their duty stations immediately. I turned to Elsie and said, "Here's the keys to my car. Take this, as I need to go to Japan. I'll be back in two weeks." That is how confident we were at the time.

I was scheduled to qualify for carrier landings on the USS *Saratoga* on Sunday, December 7. But when the Japanese hit Pearl Harbor, the *Saratoga* cancelled qualification landings and left the next morning. This delay in my qualifications meant a three-month postponement for me to get to the Pacific. I thought, "If only the Japanese had held Pearl Harbor off for just one more week, I would be satisfying my itch now and be out there aboard a carrier."

We had to wait for a carrier to come around from the Atlantic. It was the USS *Hornet*. The *Hornet* arrived at San Diego in March, and I became qualified for carrier duty. This required making three landings.

Any pilot that had trouble making three landings was reassigned to other types of duty. Just after we qualified, the *Hornet* sailed to San Francisco Bay to load B-25s and the Doolittle crews for the raid on Tokyo in April.

Boarding the *Hornet*, the sister ship of the USS *Enterprise* and the USS *Yorktown*, was made at the dock at North Island. We were to be at sea for a couple of days flying the aircraft already on board. I was concerned about how my body would react to being at sea. Would I become seasick? No, there wasn't the slightest reaction in my stomach, nor had there ever been during flying. However, when we were at last put back on terra firma, my legs seemed to sense that the ground was rolling just as the ship had. I succeeded in making three landings with three approaches, proving we had been well trained at North Island. I don't recall any other pilots having difficulties in making landing qualifications either. Not a single flyer had to be *shot down*.

In March 1942, our group of thirty took a train to San Francisco and boarded the liner *President Grant* for transport to Honolulu. The voyage was great, but we were totally dumbstruck as we pulled into Pearl Harbor and saw all of our ships that had been sunk. The first several days and nights, I stayed at Ford Island in the officers' quarters near where the *Arizona* was sunk. I could walk right out in the front yard and see the array of battleships bottoms up, on their sides or under water.

We flew training flights out of Ford Island before being transferred over to Kaneohe Naval Air Station on the eastern coast of Oahu. By that time the *Saratoga* had taken its first fish (a torpedo) and had gone back to the West Coast to be repaired. The *Sara* left some of the squadrons at Kaneohe, and I was assigned to her Bombing Squadron 3 there.

Because of the limited number of carrier pilots, each time the Navy lost a carrier, many of those pilots had to go back to the States to assist in training new air groups on the West Coast. There were few, if any, other replacement pilots coming out to the fleet until our group, which was the first new group to arrive overseas that had had advanced carrier training and was qualified for carrier landings. Our pilots were moved around from squadron to squadron and carrier to carrier. I served in

Bombing 3, 5, 6, and 10. Eventually we met every carrier pilot left in the Pacific, with eighty to one hundred per carrier and only three or four carriers. Pilots are very gregarious, as you may know, and it was easy to meet others. Within ten minutes of meeting a new pilot, it was as if you'd known him all your life.

Many of the guys thought they weren't going to live to see the end of the war. They thought the odds were against them and that the Japanese would carry the war on until eternity. I never entertained those thoughts, but a lot of men talked about it. I just shrugged off those conversations. Even so, when you were off duty, you immediately struck up strong friendships because we were all in the same boat together.

I was attached to Bombing 3 at Kaneohe, when one day the Navy needed five pilots immediately for the South Pacific. Officials at Kaneohe Air Station decided to send the first five pilots, then in the air, that landed. I was the sixth plane and was always disappointed thereafter. I was totally eager to get into action, feeling that the US couldn't win the war without me.

Within thirty minutes, the five pilots were flown over to Hickam Field, put in a B-17, and flown toward the South Pacific. Upon arrival there, they were put aboard the USS *Yorktown* and the USS *Lexington*. Within a day or two, the *Lexington* was sunk. I could forget going to where I had been assigned upon getting my wings. To the *Lexington*, that is.

· ❀ ·

PEARL HARBOR AND CORAL SEA

The attack at Pearl Harbor commenced at 7:48 a.m. Hawaiian Time, on Sunday, December 7, 1941. The base was attacked by 353 Japanese aircraft, including fighters, level and dive bombers, and torpedo bombers launched in two waves from six aircraft carriers. Eight US Navy battleships were moored at Pearl. All were damaged, four were sunk. All but the USS *Arizona* were later raised, and six were returned to service and went on to fight in the war. The Japanese also sank or damaged three cruisers, three destroyers, an anti-aircraft training ship, and one minelayer. A total of 188 US aircraft were destroyed; 2,403 Americans were killed, and 1,178 others were wounded. As naval historian Samuel Eliot Morison noted, the damage to the Pacific Fleet at Pearl Harbor left the United States with "a two-ocean war to wage with a less than one-ocean Navy."[5]

All, however, was not lost in this brutal surprise attack. Vital base installations such as the power station, dry dock, shipyard, maintenance, and fuel and torpedo storage facilities, as well as the submarine piers and headquarters building—also home of the intelligence section—were not attacked. These facilities were critically important to the ability of America to wage war against Japan.

Elsewhere in the Pacific, Allied forces were routed by the Japanese as they expanded their defensive perimeter. Wake Island, Manila and the Philippines, and Singapore fell within the first few months. In early spring 1942, the Japanese decided to invade and occupy Port Moresby in New Guinea and Tulagi in the southeastern Solomon Islands. The Japanese covering fleet for the invasion forces consisted of two fleet carriers and a light carrier. The US learned of the Japanese plan through signals intelligence and sent two US Navy carrier task forces and a joint Australian-American cruiser force to oppose the offensive, under the overall command of US Rear Adm. Frank J. Fletcher. The opposing forces grappled from May 4-8, 1942 in what would become the Battle of the Coral Sea.

Following surprise attacks by aircraft from the USS *Yorktown* on Japanese invasion troops and supporting warships, the Japanese fleet carriers advanced toward the Coral Sea with the intention of locating and destroying the Allied naval forces. On the evening of 6 May, the two carrier forces closed with each other, unbeknownst to anyone. On May 7, both sides launched airstrikes, with the US sinking the Japanese light carrier *Shōhō* and the Japanese sinking a US destroyer and heavily

---

5   Samuel Eliot Morison, *History of the United States Naval Operations in World War II, Vol. III: The Rising Sun in the Pacific, 1931-April 1942*, Boston: Little, Brown, 1948, 209.

damaging a fleet oiler, which was later scuttled. The next day, each side found and attacked the other's fleet carriers, with the Japanese fleet carrier *Shōkaku* damaged, the US fleet carrier *Lexington* critically damaged and later scuttled, and the *Yorktown* damaged. With both sides having suffered heavy losses in aircraft and carriers damaged or sunk, the two forces disengaged and retired from the area. Because of the loss of carrier air cover, the Japanese commander recalled the Port Moresby invasion fleet, setting the stage for the Solomons Islands campaign two months later.[6]

But first there would be a battle royal surrounding another island: Midway.

---

6   Morison, *History of the United States Naval Operations in World War II, Vol. IV: Coral Sea, Midway and Submarine Actions, May 1942 – August 1942*, Boston: Little Brown, 1949, 25-64; John B. Lundstrom, *The First Team: Pacific Naval Air Combat from Pearl Harbor to Midway*, Annapolis: Naval Institute Press, 1984, 135-153, 163-167, 188-190.

UNITED STATES NAVAL CHRONOLOGY WORLD WAR II

DECEMBER 1941

7 SUN. Japanese carrier-based horizontal bombers, dive bombers, torpedo bombers, and fighters totaling 360 aircraft from naval Striking Force (Vice Adm. Nagumo) heavily attack ships of the United States Pacific Fleet and installations at **Pearl Harbor** and other places on Oahu, T. H. Four battleships, 1 minelayer, and 1 target ship are sunk; 4 battleships, 3 cruisers, 3 destroyers, 1 seaplane tender, and 1 repair ship are damaged. Navy Yard and Naval Base, Pearl Harbor; Naval Air Station, Ford Island; Naval Patrol Plane Station, Kaneohe; Marine Corps airfield, Ewa; Army airfields Hickam, Wheeler, and Bellows are damaged; 188 Naval and Army aircraft are destroyed.

KILLED OR MISSING:

Navy 2,004
Marine Corps 108
Army 222

WOUNDED:

Navy 912
Marine Corps. 75
Army 360

President orders mobilization.
Japanese declaration of war reaches Washington, DC

UNITED STATES NAVAL VESSELS SUNK BY AIR ATTACK, PEARL HARBOR:

•Battleship *Oklahoma* (BB-37)
•Battleship *Arizona* (BB-39)

UNITED STATES NAVAL VESSELS SUNK BY AIR ATTACK, PEARL HARBOR (CONT.):
- Battleship *California* (BB-44)
- Battleship *West Virginia* (BB-48)
- Minelayer *Ogala* (CM-4)
- Target ship *Utah* (AG-16)

[All ships sunk, except Arizona, Oklahoma, and Utah, were raised, repaired, and subsequently returned to service.]

UNITED STATES NAVAL VESSELS DAMAGED, PEARL HARBOR:
- Battleship *Nevada* (BB-36)
- Battleship *Pennsylvania* (BB-38)
- Battleship *Tennessee* (BB-43)
- Battleship *Maryland* (BB-46)
- Light cruiser *Raleigh* (CL-7)
- Light cruiser *Honolulu* (CL-48)
- Light cruiser *Helena* (CL-50)
- Destroyer *Cassin* (DD-372)
- Destroyer *Shaw* (DD-373)
- Destroyer *Downes* (DD-375)
- Seaplane tender *Curtiss* (AV-4)
- Repair ship *Vestal* (AR-4)

JAPANESE NAVAL VESSELS LOST:
- 5 midget submarines

8 MON. United States declares war on Japan.

UNITED STATES NAVAL CHRONOLOGY WORLD WAR II

MAY 1942

4 MON. Battle of the Coral Sea (4-8 May) commences with an air strike on Tulagi, Solomon Islands, by United States carrier-based aircraft. Allied naval forces (Rear Adm. F. J. Fletcher) comprise Attack Group (Rear Adm. T. C. Kinkaid) of cruisers and destroyers and Carrier Group (Rear Adm. A. W. Fitch, USN) consisting of carriers *Lexington* (CV-2) and *Yorktown* (CV-5) with destroyers.

UNITED STATES NAVAL VESSEL SUNK:
- Minesweeper *Tanager* (AM-5), by coastal defense guns

JAPANESE NAVAL VESSEL SUNK:
- Destroyer *Kikuzuki*, by carrier-based aircraft

5 TUE. Rear Adm. F. J. Fletcher's Allied force, after fueling, changes course to intercept Japanese Port Moresby Invasion Group.

6 WED. Rear Adm. F. J. Fletcher's Allied force steams on course to intercept Japanese Port Moresby Invasion Group. (Corregidor and Manila Bay forts, P. I., surrender to the Japanese.)

7 THU. Rear Adm. F. J. Fletcher's Allied force turns north to engage Japanese Attack Group. Carrier aircraft attack Japanese Support Group and sink aircraft carrier Shoho.

UNITED STATES NAVAL VESSEL SUNK:
- Destroyer *Sims* (DD-409), by dive bomber

UNITED STATES NAVAL VESSEL DAMAGED:
- Oiler *Neosho* (AO-23), by dive bomber and sunk by United States forces

JAPANESE NAVAL VESSEL SUNK:
- Carrier *Shoho*, by carrier-based aircraft

8 FRI. Carrier *Lexington* (CV-2) search aircraft sight Japanese carriers *Shokaku* and *Zuikaku*. Rear Adm. F. J. Fletcher's carrier aircraft damage *Shokaku* and force her retirement. At the same time, Japanese aircraft hit carriers *Yorktown* (CV-5) and Lexington (CV-2), damaging the latter to such an extent that destroyer *Phelps* (DD-360) is ordered to sink her.

UNITED STATES NAVAL VESSEL SUNK:
- Carrier *Lexington* (CV-2), severely damaged by carrier-based torpedo bombers and sunk by United States forces

UNITED STATES NAVAL VESSEL DAMAGED:
- Carrier *Yorktown* (CV-5), by carrier-based dive bombers.

One must control his fear. The flier has to control his mind, because if fear comes in, then he is in trouble. I was never without fear, but I never let fear conquer my mind and emotions. By the time I went aboard the Yorktown, I'd conquered my plane. My body and the plane were totally one.

—Lt. Cdr. Robert "Hoot" Gibson

MIDWAY

BATTLE OF MIDWAY

June 4-6, 1942

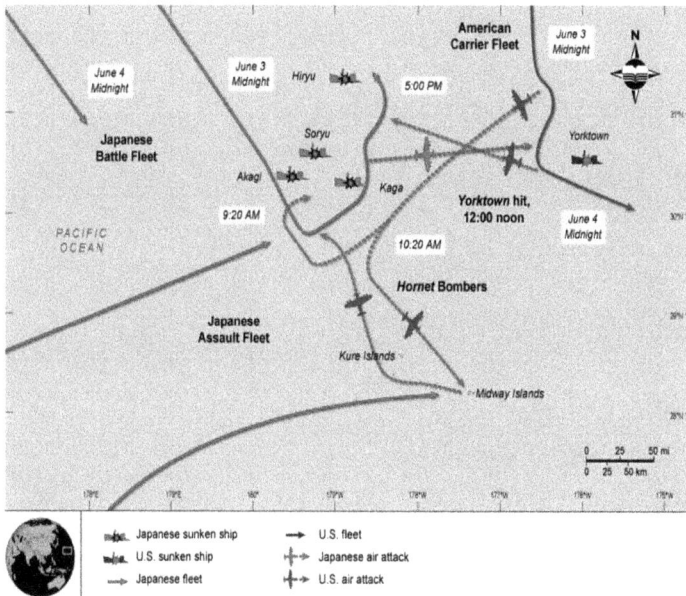

*Japanese battle and assault fleets and American carrier
fleet movements at Battle of Midway[7]*

---

7   Map image located at https://www.bhs-lmc.org/world-war-ii-turning-point-battles.

CHAPTER THREE

MIDWAY

Bombing Five, USS Yorktown (CV-5)
"Please push me overboard"

USS Yorktown (CV-5) in a dry dock at the
Pearl Harbor Naval Shipyard May 29, 1942 (US Navy)

SPRINGING THE TRAP

THE BATTLE OF Midway took place June 4-7, 1942, six months after
Japan's attack on Pearl Harbor and one month after the Battle of the

Coral Sea. The US Navy under Admirals Chester W. Nimitz, Frank J. Fletcher, and Raymond A. Spruance and their three carrier groups faced an attacking four-carrier fleet of the Imperial Japanese Navy under Admirals Yamamoto, Nagumo, and Kondō near Midway Atoll.

The Japanese were hoping to lure the American aircraft carriers into a trap. Occupying Midway Island was part of an overall *barrier* strategy to extend Japan's defensive perimeter in response to the Doolittle air raid on Tokyo. They also were setting the stage for further attacks against Fiji, Samoa, and Hawaii itself. The Japanese made faulty assumptions of the American reaction to the attack on Pearl Harbor and poor initial dispositions weighed heavily against the Japanese fleet. Most significantly, US Navy cryptographers were able to determine the date and location of the planned attack, enabling the US Navy to prepare its own ambush.

· ❀ ·

"CALCULATED RISK"

"In carrying out the tasks assigned . . . you will be governed by the principle of calculated risk, which you shall interpret to mean the avoidance of exposure to attack superior enemy forces without good prospect of inflicting, as a result of such exposure, greater damage to the enemy."

—Order from Admiral Nimitz to Task Force Commanders
—Battle of Midway

· ❀ ·

INTO THE FRAY

Just before the Battle of Midway, the Battle of the Coral Sea took place May 8, 1942. During the battle, the carrier *Yorktown* was badly damaged and limped back to Pearl Harbor. Crews were assigned to work twenty-four hours a day repairing damage on the *Yorktown* to enable it to depart within a very few days for Midway to fight again.

The *Yorktown* wasn't the only casualty at Coral Sea. We lost the *Lexington* and I lost one of my best buddies, Ensign Davis Elliott "Red" Chaffee. He was one of my closest original E-base and flight training friends. Red was assigned to Bombing 5 on the *Yorktown* at the Battle of Coral Sea. His plane suffered heavy damage after he completed his dive on *Shokaku*. He was probably wounded, as he was not communicating and his rear gunner was already dead from a round that had hit him in the head. His wing blew off, after which he was last seen going in. His tail section was seen floating but there was no sign of life. I took Chaffee's loss personally as I had pushed him through flight training in Florida.[8]

· ❀ ·

USS *CHAFFEE*

Chaffee was posthumously awarded the Navy Cross and a Destroyer Escort (DE-230) launched in 1943 was named after him. The USS *Chaffee* was luckier than its namesake. Assigned to patrol in Lingayen Gulf, the *Chaffee* underwent a unique experience on January 23,1945, when a Japanese Mitsubishi G4M "Betty" dropped an aerial torpedo that passed through her bow without exploding or causing any injuries to her crew. The propeller from the torpedo was recovered in the bow of the ship. It is in the collection of the National Museum of the United States Navy at the Washington Navy Yard, Washington, DC.

· ❀ ·

USS *YORKTOWN*

"The hastily patched Yorktown *slipped out of dry dock on May 29. When the squadrons flew out to the carrier the next day, nearly half*

---

8   Moore, *Hell's Island*, 135-136.

*of the VB-5 pilots were making their first landings . . . The Dauntless landings on **Yorktown** went smoothly on the first day out of Pearl. One of the VF-3 rookies, however, bounced upon touchdown and smashed into the back of another Wildcat. His propeller chopped through the cockpit of Lieutenant Don Lovelace's F4F, killing the fighter squadron executive officer."*[9]

• ✿ •

I was assigned to Bombing 5 (VB-5)[10] on board *Yorktown*. At Ford Island, I jumped into an SBD and flew out to rendezvous with the air group and land aboard the *Yorktown*, where I first met the pilots in the bombing squadron. It was only a few days until the *Yorktown* was sunk. I was in the squadron one week, but what an experience. As to our mission before Midway, we were told nothing. We were expendable.

• ✿ •

In his epic Pacific War trilogy, author Ian Toll sets the stage for the Battle of Midway as follows:

> For the American Task Forces, pushing north from Oahu through rough seas and biting winds, the first three days of June had brought cold, wet air and a gray, dirty sky. Throughout the long hours of daylight, the ships zigzagged prodigiously, a measure against submarines. They steamed at twenty knots, rising and plunging through white-flecked chop, heeling sharply as they turned in unison every few miles. . . .

---

9   Moore, *Pacific Payback: The Carrier Aviators Who Avenged Pearl Harbor at the Battle of Midway*, New York: NAL Caliber/Penguin Random House, 2015, 169 (hereafter "Pacific Payback").

10   Bombing 5 (VB-5) [Lt. Wallace C. Short, Jr. commanding] was re-designated Scouting 5 (VS-5) when the Saratoga's Bombing 3 (VB-3) [Lt. Cmdr. Maxwell F. Leslie commanding] joined the Yorktown Air Group.

The flyboys were shaken awake[11] and sent to flight quarters in the small hours of the morning [of June 4]. Reveille for the torpedo aircrews was at 3 a.m. They pulled on their flight suits and filed down to the mess hall for coffee and breakfast. On the *Yorktown* they were served steak and eggs, much better than the usual fare, and one torpedo airman was overheard joking that it was a "feast for condemned men." After eating they drifted back to their ready rooms, where the flight rosters were "grease-penciled on the Plexiglas schedule board."

Before first light, the F4Fs of the combat air patrols took off, and ten scout bombers were sent off the *Yorktown* to fly search patterns to the north. The main airstrike was kept on deck, however—Fletcher had decided to close the distance on the enemy, and wait for a definite sighting report before sending the attack planes on their way.

The morning was fair, with fresh, cool air and a beautiful blue sky dotted with small, fleecy clouds. Visibility was superb.[12]

· 🍁 ·

FIRST TASTE

One thing I recall about the *Yorktown* was that the food was great. Special attention had been given at Pearl Harbor to supply the best of foods, as the cruise was expected to be short, if not sweet. We may have been expendable, but we had steak and eggs for breakfast—the very finest food. Off the wardroom was the officers' little lounge where waiters would present us with cigars and cigarettes. We had our own silver napkin rings and linen napkins, and tablecloths, real silverware,

---

11   As new rookies in the Yorktown's bombing squadron, Hoot, Jerry Richey, and John Bridgers were ordered to wake up the other pilots forty minutes before their flight time. Moore, Pacific Payback, 173.

12   Ian W. Toll, *Pacific Crucible: War at Sea in the Pacific, 1941-1942*, New York: Norton, 2012, 417-419 (hereafter *Pacific Crucible*).

and beautiful plates. *Yorktown* was a high-class outfit. My stateroom had covering on the deck and curtains on the port hole. After the vicious fires resulting from bombing at Midway, no other Navy ship went to sea with such luxuries. But my duty on the *Yorktown* was short. I'd had three or four flights. We were sunk on June 4, and I had gone on board May 28.

I had total respect for a propeller. My mind established a strict block against ever exposing any part of me within the trajectory of a propeller. On the first pre-dawn flight from the *Yorktown* en route to Midway, I was held up as the call came, "Pilots, man your planes." Arriving on the flight deck under a rainy, dark night, I found all aircraft engines running, and I had to make it three rows back to board my plane. The prop blasts from the propellers, the ship speeding and running into the wind, and a plotting board under my arms acting as a sail, I knew I was in grave danger. While crawling under the wings of planes, I watched my plotting board[13] sail into the sea. Climbing into my plane, I noticed 90 percent of my right wing hanging sixty-five feet above the water. I thought, "Going into battle can't be much worse than this."

The morning of the Battle of Midway, my plane was on the hangar deck. I was assigned to fly on the early-morning search. Again, and for the last time, we had steak and eggs for breakfast. It was still dark outside when I went to the ready room and then back to the hangar deck, got into my plane, started it up, and taxied up the elevator, took off, and came back aboard about 0930 from the search—a normal search of 250 miles.

• ❖ •

---

13   "Each aviator worked on his own navigational plotting board, and entered new data forwarded from AirPlot by teleprinter. He constantly checked and rechecked the position, course, and speed of the enemy fleet and of his own ship. He added corrections for the strength and direction of the wind, and for the magnetic deviations on his compass readings. He reckoned flight times and fuel consumption, and plotted his return course to 'Point Option,' where he was to find his carrier at the end of his flight." Toll, *Pacific Crucible*, 417-418.

"At 0430, the usual one-half hour before daylight, [Rear Admiral Frank Jack] Fletcher, who had steamed an easterly course in the early morning hours of the night, changed his axis and course to south and west at a speed calculated to bring him two hundred miles east of Midway at dawn. He launched a search group of ten SBD scouts to cover the northern sector and the ocean area to the westward for a distance of two hundred miles."[14]

. ❊ .

SCOUTING 101

The protocol for this situation did not exact a high degree of technical knowhow, just situational awareness. Scouting entailed filing contact reports, bombing a target, and staying alive.

The procedure went like this: First, you would write a report on your kneepad, which was one part of our flying gear. On the pad you would describe the makeup of the Japanese fleet, its speed, direction, and the latitude-longitude. This was computed as reasonably accurate so you could rely upon your own skill of staying alive over an endless ocean. Then there was your plotting-board, a circular slide-rule, which showed you where you were located. Experience enabled you to judge the distance and direction from you to the enemy. You penciled that information onto the plotting-board grid that then gave the position of the fleet. Reading the direction of movement could easily be extrapolated in relation to your own compass heading.

The speed of the fleet was discernable by the memory bank in your head that read the size of a ship's wake, produced as the ship traveled through the seas. A certain sized wake said that the ship was moving at twenty, twenty-five or thirty knots. If you were a serious student, you could be accurate within a knot or two. If not, you had no business

14   Vice Admiral William Ward "Poco" Smith, *Midway: Turning Point of the Pacific*, New York: Thomas Y. Crowell, 1966, 77.

being there and might end up suffering mistakes in your own dead reckoning over an unimaginable span of water. There were no railroad tracks to fly down, as the Navy teased the Army.

You then tore off the message sheet, attached it by a clothes pin to a thin wire on a pulley, and moved the message to the rear cockpit for the radioman-gunner to read and translate into Morse Code by using the required key, also furnished for the transmission of radio messages. The clothesline pulley arrangement was so successful that it would also work in reverse, so that the radioman could decipher an incoming Morse code message, write the message down on his knee pad and pull the line for delivery to be read by you. High technology.

• ✻ •

FIRST STRIKE

"The Yorktown *launched her attack squadrons between 0838 and 0906. Fletcher, in launching his attack, held Squadron VS-5, composed of nineteen SBDs, in reserve, available for scouting or dive-bombing . . . The pilots . . . wanted to be in on this fight. They could not understand why they were held back."[15]*

Prior to my landing back on board from my assigned search sector, the *Yorktown* had launched the first strike group. When I came aboard, I wasn't scheduled to fly until the strike group came back, on the second strike. At the same time the strike group was due back, the Japanese hit us. The Japanese air group more or less followed our airplanes back; although some say a Japanese cruiser search plane discovered the *Yorktown* about mid-morning. The time the Japanese hit us was late in the morning and they scored three times in a dive-bombing attack.

---

15   Smith, 95.

Smoke pours from the USS Yorktown (CV-5) after being
hit in the boilers by Japanese dive bombers at Midway.
(Photographer 2nd Class William G. Roy—US Navy)

• ❖ •

*"Only seven dive-bombers got through the American fighters to
attack the* Yorktown, *but those seven pilots were among the first
team of the Japanese carrier air force, and they knew their business
... The first Aichi to dive was hit by flak right as it dropped its bomb—
it exploded and broke into three flaming pieces that splashed into
the ship's wake. But the pilot's aim was true—the cartwheeling bomb
struck the deck just aft of the* Yorktown's *island structure. The blast
decimated the crew of the 1.1 inch antiaircraft mount that had just
splashed the same plane that had dropped the bomb."*[16]

• ❖ •

---

16   Toll, *Pacific Crucible*, 445.

STARK TERROR

I had been in the ready room for the first attack. Upon cessation, I ran up the one flight of stairs to the flight deck, the door of which came out of the island structure. There I faced a large pond of blood twenty feet across where a dozen men had been killed. The first thing I noticed was that the pool of blood was flowing away from the direction that the ship was violently turning. In tight turns the ship heels over away from the turn and the blood was following.

I quickly turned the corner behind the island only to look down into the catwalk running four feet lower than the flight deck. There I saw and heard the cry of an old sailor lying on the catwalk. "Please push me overboard." I was transfixed a second time within seconds, as the man was also lying in a pool of his own blood and had both legs missing. I was experiencing stark terror and as I stood immobile, I saw him grab the stanchion cable with one hand, and with superhuman strength pulled himself overboard into the sea and death. This was one of the most heroic acts I saw during the war.

• ❧ •

"Airmen in the ready room [were] gasping and teary eyed . . . look[ing] around in the fresh air on the open flight deck . . . The 1.1 inch mount aft of the island, which had been struck directly, was a terrible sight. . . 'a mass of bloody flesh encased in shredded denim. On the 20 mm battery on the catwalk, the gunner's head had been blown off but his body remained strapped securely into the chair.'"[17]

---

17   Toll, *Pacific Crucible*, 446.

**Rough landings: Repairs in the flight deck on *Yorktown*.
(US Naval Institute)**

Without any assigned duties I wandered the flight and hangar decks trying to give a hand with water hoses. As the fires were raging, the crew started throwing all the mattresses and other combustibles overboard.

In between the first and second attacks I saw the admiral and his staff transfer from the *Yorktown* to a cruiser. His name was Frank "Black Jack" Fletcher. Although he won the Medal of Honor at Veracruz in Mexico in 1914 when a lieutenant, he was over the hill at Midway. We had control of the fires from the bombs and were getting underway, smartly as they say, but here was our leader, the admiral, jumping ship. What an example.

• ❧ •

To add to the ignominious image, Fletcher signaled Rear Admiral Smith on the heavy cruiser *Astoria* to send a boat for himself and his staff. Poco Smith describes that:

"The *Astoria* lowered a motor whaleboat which lost no time in reaching the stricken carrier. It is a long way from a carrier's deck to the sea below. It's possible to jump overboard, but hazardous, so Fletcher's staff went hand-over-hand down ropes thrown from the flight deck. Black Jack gave it a try but had to admit his arm muscles hadn't had sufficient exercise for some time. A bowline was secured beneath his arms, and he was lowered into the boat."[18]

· ✿ ·

Surprisingly, Black Jack was then on the *Enterprise*, as was I, at the invasion of Guadalcanal, two months later. Not surprisingly to me, Black Jack abandoned Admiral Turner and his invasion forces after the first night, leaving Turner, his supplies, and thousands of men unprotected. Fletcher coined one of many feeble excuses, "I must retire to refuel." Why hadn't he brought the tanker up to him to refuel while keeping a protective covering over Turner and the First Marine Division? What a coward. I squawked to my CO and asked him to let me take a flight of planes over to Guadalcanal to give some protection. I told Ray Davis, the CO, my opinion of Fletcher from the fink-out at Midway. After abandoning Turner, Fletcher was replaced and never commanded in combat again during the war.

· ✿ ·

SECOND ATTACK

"At about 1442, Yorktown *dodged two torpedoes but two others hit and exploded, breaching most of the fuel tanks on her port side, jamming the rudder, severing all power connections, and causing an immediate list of 17 degrees, which increased to about 26 degrees in the next 20 minutes.... Captain Buckmaster ... feared the* Yorktown

---

18   Smith, 116.

was about to capsize. A few minutes before 1500 he ordered 'Abandon Ship.' Four destroyers closed to take off the crew or pick them up in the water. . . . Floating bluejackets amused each other by calling 'Taxi! Taxi!' and thumbing imaginary rides at drifting debris; strains of the 'Beer Barrel Polka' floated from one raft full of officers and men.'[19]

· ❀ ·

WHERE IS SANCHO PANZA
WHEN YOU NEED HIM?

When the second attack came at Midway, with torpedo planes, I found myself near my stateroom. Dashing into a room, I flopped down on the bottom bunk. I was sort of scared, to put it mildly. The mattress was gone as well so I lay on the springs face down still wearing my Mae West life jacket.

The *Yorktown* was hit by two torpedoes. That shook the ship radically, as if our entire ship were a baby rattle. The lights went out, and the room filled with smoke. As I got up, the toggle strings on the Mae West entangled in the coil springs and the springs came up with me and I hit the top bunk. I was kind of like Don Quixote fighting the windmill, fighting those springs and wanting to get out of there. With adrenalin flowing in superman quantities, I tore myself loose and ran out on to the weather deck underneath the flight deck.

The ship was listing, and I wanted my mother. I didn't like it. The ship was listing so much to port I went to the starboard—the high side—somehow, I thought if went to the other side it might tip the ship over. A cook frantically ran up beside me, looked about, and said, "This deck is way too hot for my feet" and jumped overboard.

The ship's bullhorn announced, "Abandon Ship!"

· ❀ ·

19   Morison, *Coral Sea, Midway and Submarine Actions, May 1942 – August 1942,* 135-136 (citing story by petty officer Harvey Wilder in *Atlantic Journal* 16 Sept. 1942).

"Almost as if consciously striving to maintain order in the face of catastrophe, most of the crew members removed their shoes before going over the side and, for some unspoken reason, left them arranged in neat rows on the flight deck."[20]

· ❋ ·

HELPING HANDS

I grabbed a line that had been tossed over and slid to the ocean. I didn't think to lock my feet, so I burned my hands on the rope. Then I dropped into the water, but as I tried to swim away the waves kept knocking me back against the hull of the ship. The surface of the water was covered with oil. They had taught us that in this situation, you should dive under the water and swim as far as you could before you came up to get a breath of air and went under water again.

Each time I came up a wave would knock me back against the ship. This went on for an eternity—three or four times—then a helping hand came out of a raft and pulled me aboard.

USS *Yorktown* (CV-5) listing 23 degrees to port following Japanese attack on June 4, 1942. Hoot Gibson possibly in lower right of photo. (US Navy)

---

20   Smith, 123.

The helping hand was that of a commander, a man named Arnold. He was the air officer on the *Yorktown*. About a year and a half later, when I came back to San Francisco, Arnold was one of the officers who decided what they were going to do with our group of pilots. Each pilot was interviewed by a board and then assigned. I requested to go to Pensacola or one of the training centers to spend some time training pilots. On the reviewing board was now Captain Arnold. He looked at me and said, "You look familiar."

I said, "Yes, remember at Midway? You were the man who pulled me out of the water. I know you've been back in the States since then. I've been through five or six battles since then and I'd like to spend a little time here and see a football game."

He laughed and I went outside the room. Shortly, I was told the Navy had assigned me to Corpus Christi Naval Air Station.

* 🎖 *

USS *BALCH*

The USS *Balch* (DD-363), at right, picking up survivors from the *Yorktown* on the afternoon of June 4. (US Naval Institute)

After that first helping hand, I made it safely on board the USS *Balch*, a *Farragut*-class destroyer. In addition to its normal complement of men, there were hundreds of survivors from *Yorktown*. This included the soon-to-be-dead, the wounded, and the later-to-be-dead. The only space I could find to spend the night was sitting on the bench by the bulkhead in the Officer's Wardroom. The dining table was not used for dining that night, though. I'm not sure there was any such thing as dining anywhere on ship, but instead it was utilized as the operating table throughout the night.

There was no sleeping for me throughout that night at Midway. I watched as a young Navy doctor named Lee handled the most complex situations. By morning the stench of medicine and the stronger smell of death was emblazoned on my senses. Never again would I forget the smell of death.

*   ❦   *

"The complement assigned a modern destroyer of the time was 250 officers and men; messing and berthing facilities were provided for that number only, and there was no such thing as idle space in a ship designed for fighting. Balch found herself with 541 passengers. A large percentage of those rescued were coated with sticky, foul-odored fuel oil. They had brought with them nothing but the wet, stained, and tattered clothes in which they stood."[21]

Hoot and *Yorktown* friends crowd onto the USS *Balch* late afternoon June 4, 1942. (US Navy)

---

21   Smith, 123.

RESULTS

After Midway, the Japanese fleet had sulked back to Japan in such secrecy that the wounded were taken ashore at night in well-guarded ports. It was the first Japanese defeat in modern times, and the magnitude of it was carefully kept secret from the Japanese nation until long after the war was over. Within the Japanese Navy the truth could not be disguised; the carriers and planes might be replaced in time, but the pilots could never be. They were the flower of the peacetime training program: a regime of the utmost rigor, which only the most gifted flyer survived.

Never again would Japan have time to train such men as these original pilots who had had six or more years of experience fighting the war in China. They were part of approximately 100 of their leading pilots. A good many of them were killed at the Battle of Midway and by the end of 1942, we found that practically all the first-line pilots had been killed in the subsequent battles that year.

"The efforts and sacrifices of the Army, Navy, and Marine Corps forces involved in the Battle of Midway have been crowned with glorious success and I firmly believe have already changed the course of the war."

—Admiral Chester Nimitz

MIRACLE AT MIDWAY

At Midway, the US Navy inflicted devastating damage on the Japanese fleet that rendered their aircraft carriers irreparable. It was a stunning and decisive blow to the Japanese fleet. Four Japanese and three American

aircraft carriers participated in the battle. The four Japanese fleet carriers—
Akagi, Kaga, Sōryū and Hiryū, part of the six-carrier force that had attacked
Pearl Harbor six months earlier—were sunk, as was the heavy cruiser
Mikuma. The US lost the carrier *Yorktown* and the destroyer *Hammann,*
while the carriers USS *Enterprise* and USS *Hornet* survived the battle
fully intact.

The Japanese march had been checked for the first time in the war.

More trouble was brewing in the South Pacific as Japan moved to
throttle and isolate Australia and the Allied forces under MacArthur.
The Japanese moved toward the Solomon Islands to establish an airfield
from which to strike the Allied supply lines and to expand their defensive
perimeter.

UNITED STATES NAVAL CHRONOLOGY WORLD WAR II

JUNE 1942

2 TUE. Two carrier task forces (Rear Adm. F. J. Fletcher and Rear Adm. R. A. Spruance) rendezvous about 350 miles northeast of Midway Island.

3 WED. Midway-based aircraft locate and attack transports of Japanese Combined Fleet (Admiral Yamamoto) about 600 miles west of Midway Island.

4 THU. Battle of Midway (4-6 June) opens as aircraft from four Japanese carriers strike Midway Island installations, which are defended by Marine and Army aircraft. Carrier task forces (Rear Adm. F. J. Fletcher and Rear Adm. R. A. Spruance) launch aircraft from carriers *Enterprise* (CV-6), *Hornet* (CV-8) and *Yorktown* (CV-5), which hit four Japanese carriers. Yorktown is disabled by Japanese carrier aircraft. Admiral Yamamoto abandons midway invasion plans and retires westward.

UNITED STATES NAVAL VESSEL DAMAGED/SUNK:
•Carrier *Yorktown* (CV-5), by carrier-based aircraft

JAPANESE NAVAL VESSELS SUNK:
•Carrier *Kaga*, by carrier-based aircraft
•Carrier *Soryu*, by carrier-based aircraft and submarine Nautilus
(SS-168)

5 FRI. Carrier task force (Rear Adm. R. A. Spruance) pursues Japanese fleet westward.

JAPANESE NAVAL VESSELS SUNK:
• Carrier *Akagi*, damaged by carrier-based aircraft, sunk by own forces
• Carrier *Hiryu*, damaged by carrier-based aircraft, sunk by own forces

6 SAT. Aircraft from carriers *Enterprise* (CV-6) and *Hornet* (CV-8) attack Japanese force retiring from midway. After recovering aircraft, United States force changes course eastward to refuel and breaks contact with the enemy.

UNITED STATES NAVAL VESSEL SUNK:
• Destroyer *Hammann* (DD-412), by submarine torpedo

JAPANESE NAVAL VESSEL SUNK:
• Heavy cruiser *Mikuma*, by naval carrier-based aircraft and
Marine aircraft

GUADALCANAL

THE BATTLE FOR GUADALCANAL

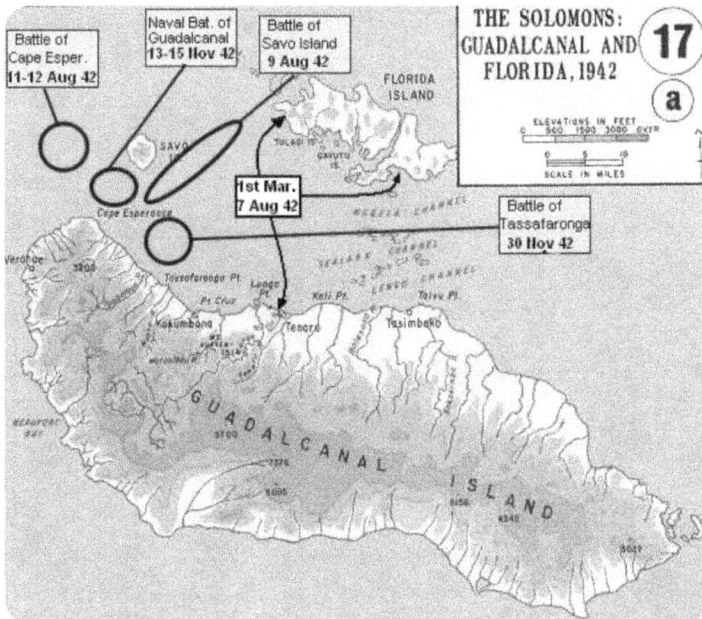

**Guadalcanal and the Solomon Islands Campaign
(August to November, 1942)[22]**

Operation Watchtower: Task One—
Seize Guadalcanal Island, Tulagi, and adjacent positions.

---

22   Guadalcanal Island. Map annotated by Bradipus. Battles Around Guadalcanal
1942. Casta-MAP_Guadalcanal-battles3.jpg

CHAPTER FOUR

GUADALCANAL

Bombing Six, USS Enterprise *(CV-6)*
"A whooee-a-whooee"

Hoot Gibson (left) and his rear gunner Cliff Schindele, 1942

THE SOUTH PACIFIC

THE SOLOMON ISLANDS campaign began with Japanese landings
and occupation of several areas in the British Solomon Islands and

Bougainville, in the Territory of New Guinea, during the first six months of 1942. The Japanese occupied these locations and began the construction of several naval and air bases with the goals of protecting the flank of the Japanese offensive in New Guinea, establishing a security barrier for the major Japanese base at Rabaul on New Britain, and providing bases for interdicting supply lines between the Allied powers of the United States and Australia and New Zealand.

Following Midway, in order to defend their communication and supply lines in the South Pacific, the US Navy and Allies supported a counteroffensive in New Guinea to isolate the Japanese base at Rabaul, and a counterattack against the Japanese in the Solomons. It was a hard and harrowing campaign for both sides. Code-named Operation Watchtower by American forces, the Battle of Guadalcanal was fought between August 7, 1942 and February 9, 1943 on and around the island of Guadalcanal. It was the first major land offensive by Allied forces against Japan.

On August 7, 1942, the US Marines landed on Guadalcanal, Tulagi, and Florida in the southern Solomon Islands, with the objective of using Guadalcanal and Tulagi as bases in supporting a campaign to eventually capture or neutralize the major Japanese base at Rabaul on New Britain. The Japanese defenders, who had occupied those islands since May 1942, were outnumbered and overwhelmed by the Allies, who captured Tulagi and Florida, as well as the airfield – later named Henderson Field – that was under construction on Guadalcanal.

Surprised by the Allied offensive, the Japanese made several attempts between August and November to retake Henderson Field. Three major land battles, seven large naval battles—five nighttime surface actions and two carrier battles—and almost daily aerial battles culminated in the decisive Naval Battle of Guadalcanal in early November, with the defeat of the last Japanese attempt to bombard Henderson Field from the sea and to land enough troops to retake it. In December, the Japanese abandoned their efforts to retake Guadalcanal, and evacuated their remaining forces by February 7, 1943 in the face of an offensive by the US Army's XIV Corps. The Battle of Rennell Island, the last major naval engagement, served to secure protection for the Japanese troops to evacuate safely.[23] Guadalcanal had earned its title of Hell's Island.[24]

· 🏵 ·

HELL'S ISLAND

"The Japanese setback at Midway had deprived them of some of their offensive capacity because of the loss of four aircraft carriers, but as the Americans soon discovered in the Solomons, Japan had great naval strength and enormous resilience. The American and Australian naval catastrophe at Savo Island in August 1942 and the desperate fighting on Guadalcanal and in Papua showed that the real war in the Pacific was just beginning to get under way."[25]

· 🏵 ·

THE SOLOMONS

I went to sea aboard the *Enterprise* on July 15, 1942. I was twenty-two years of age. The Big E was part of a task force consisting of a large new battleship and accompanying cruisers. On August 7, 1942, I was on the first pre-dawn flight—the second plane to drop a bomb in the Guadalcanal invasion. So, I was in on our first invasion in the Pacific and later in the last invasion, in Borneo, of the war.

---

23   Samuel Eliot Morison, *The Struggle for Guadalcanal, August 1942 – February 1943, History of the United States Naval Operations in World War II*, Volume V, Boston: Little, Brown, 1949, 12-16, 351-363, 371-373.

24   "Many English speakers not versed in history find it shocking that Guadalcanal does not have an actual canal. The very name suggests a fundamental dishonesty about the island—an island that, as many a writer has opined, looks like paradise but is more like Paradise Lost." Jeffrey R. Cox, *Blazing Star, Setting Sun: The Guadalcanal-Solomons Campaign, November 1942 – March 1943*. Oxford: Osprey, 2020, 22.

25   Gerhard L. Weinberg, *World in the Balance: Behind the Scenes of World War II*, University Press of New England, Hanover, N.H., 1981, 37.

· ❧ ·

THE BIG E

After I got back to Pearl Harbor from Midway, I was assigned to Bombing Six and attached to the *Enterprise*. Many of the Midway pilots on the *Enterprise* went back stateside. The loss of the *Yorktown* at Midway was partially compensated for by the return of the USS *Saratoga* to Hawaii at that same time. The Navy again had the availability of four fast carriers including the USS *Hornet* and the USS *Wasp*. Our task force moved out to sea at flank (true maximum) speed headed for the Fiji Islands to conduct practice maneuvers after rendezvousing with Navy transports loaded with Marines. As usual, I lucked out and was spared the discomfort of going through the initiation ceremonies to the King Neptune Society when crossing the Equator for the first time. I was, however, issued a certificate of accomplishing the crossing. The certificate stated *War Operations against Japan*.

At the Fiji Islands, the combined fleet of capital ships and the amphibious forces fleet conducted simulated landing, in practice for the *real McCoy*. On board our ship the pilots enjoyed passing scuttlebutt about where we were headed. The Navy was consistent in keeping the pilots in the dark, which we wondered about. Maybe it was to keep us from spilling the beans if tortured by the Japanese.

The procedure was to brief the pilots only in their Ready Room during the last thirty minutes before launching. There each pilot was given instructions for his mission, or the group was given the same instructions if there was to be a group attack. Any pilot, for example, on a search mission was expected to radio a contact report, and then automatically was expected to climb to altitude and to press home a dive attack against an enemy ship.

Before taking off for the first strike, I promised all pilots that I would sing out a phrase, over the radio, from my favorite song of that day, it was "Blues in the Night."[26] And the phrase I sang while in a Split S beginning the bomb run was, "*a whooee-a-whooee.*" My gravelly voice probably struck fear into the Japanese hearts all the way to Rabaul.

· ❧ ·

THE LANDINGS

The task forces of *Wasp*, *Saratoga,* and *Enterprise* were to support the landings of the First Marine Division on Guadalcanal and Tulagi Islands in the Solomons. The Dauntless pilots for these carrier task forces had the morning off from search duty on August 6 to prevent their planes from being spotted.[27]

· ❧ ·

DOGFIGHT

We bombed an island off Tulagi called Guavutu where the Japanese were deeply entrenched. It then became a process of flying back to the carrier to load bombs for the next sortie. When I came back to the action, it was midday and our six or eight SBDs were circling, waiting to be directed to a target. I could see a number of Bettys,[28] the twin-engine Japanese bombers far below being worked over by a group of *Enterprise* fighters, probably led by a man named Runyan, a machinist. We saw our fighters splash the enemy and few, if any, Bettys survived.

As we were headed in a westerly direction over Tulagi, I could see over the far horizon to the southeast a little dot that was coming in our direction at a high rate of speed. All of a sudden, shells from below were going by in front of me and then a 20 mm cannon shell hit me in the seat

---

26   The 1942 song had been recorded by popular artists like Dinah Shore, Woody Herman and Ella Fitzgerald and included the "whooee-a-whooee, ol'clickety-clack, I'm back on the track of blues in the night" lyrics.
27   Moore, *Hell's Island*, 195.
28   Mitsubishi G4M Type 1 Land Attack Plane ("Betty").

and exploded. It had hit my bomb, glanced up and exploded against my seat with shrapnel passing out through the radio equipment between the two cockpits.[29] Our seats were made of thick armor plate, bullet proof glass protected the front of the pilot, and the engine in front of us was also a shield. In order for a machine gun bullet to kill you or hit your body it had to come from a high front side attack. Otherwise, the pilot's four limbs were the most vulnerable. The cannon shell ricocheted from my bomb and exploded under my armored seat. The shrapnel took on renewed energy and sprayed hot jagged steel in all directions except my body. Saved by a seat, but with no time to appreciate the miracle!

At the same second that the canon shell hit me, our rear gunners [RM3c Ed Anderson and others] were firing like crazy. I looked over my shoulder and about twenty feet behind me, going straight up, was a Japanese Zero[30] in a huge ball of fire. Our rear gunners had hit him, and everyone believed the pilot was dead. I had no chance to see the Zero crash in the ocean, as we were intent upon placing our bombs where they counted, and certainly not upon our own troops. The Zero pilot recovered from his death throes by slipping the plane to extinguish the fire and was able to fly back to base. He was acclaimed as one of the leading aces of the Japanese military. Saburo Sakai was his name. One of the shell bursts blinded him in one eye. He did a miraculous job of getting the fire out and getting back to Rabaul, a four-hour flight.

* 🍁 *

A SWIFT KICK IN THE PANTS

Guadalcanal historian Eric Hammel covers Sakai's remarkable fight as follows:

---

29   "Gibson recalled, 'My seat was armor plated and the blast was directed straight upward, tearing out my radio.'" Barrett Tillman, *America's Fightingest Ship and The Men Who Helped Win World War II*, New York: Simon Schuster, 2012, 96.

30   Mitsubishi A6M Type 00 (Reisen) Carrier Fighter, Model 11 ("Zero").

Saburo Sakai spotted eight Enterprise Dauntlesses under the command of Lt. Carl Horenburger. The Dauntlesses were orbiting to provide on-call air support for Marines fighting on Tulagi and Gavutu. Sakai was coming in directly from astern, and he started firing when he was about 500 feet away from the rear SBD. A 20mm shell hit the vane of Ens. Bob Gibson's 500-pound bomb, then ricocheted upward and exploded beneath Gibson's armored seat. To Gibson, the detonation felt like a swift kick in the pants, but he was unharmed. By then several of the American gunners had responded with bursts from their twin .30 caliber machine guns. However, several others, including AOM2 Jones, could not initially bring their guns to bear on Sakai without shooting up the tails of their bombers. When Sakai turned to the right and pulled up in order to avoid colliding with the SBDs, every rearseatman could safely fire. And all of them did.

Then, Sakai's Zero began a vertical plunge toward the water. By incredible good fortune, Japan's leading ace overcame his severe head wounds and gravity to pull out at wavetop height and lurch for home. Though severely wounded and nearly blinded from severe facial and eye injuries, Sakai struggled on to complete an epic 560-mile flight home in under 5 hours.[31]

· ❀ ·

THE SOLOMONS SKEDADDLE

Bad weather allowed the Allied expeditionary force to arrive unseen by the Japanese on the night of August 6 and the following morning, taking the defenders by surprise. The landing force split into two groups, with one group assaulting Guadalcanal, and the other Tulagi, Florida, and nearby

---

31   Eric Hammel, *Guadalcanal, The Carrier Battles: The Pivotal Aircraft Carrier Battles of the Eastern Solomons and Santa Cruz.* New York: Crown, 1987, 27-29.

islands. Allied warships bombarded the invasion beaches, while US carrier aircraft bombed Japanese positions on the target islands.

During the landing operations on August 7-8, Japanese naval aircraft based at Rabaul attacked the Allied amphibious forces several times. In the air attacks over the two days, the Japanese lost thirty-six aircraft, while the US lost nineteen, both in combat and to accidents, including fourteen carrier fighters.

After these clashes, Rear Adm. Fletcher withdrew his carrier task forces from the Solomon Islands area on the evening of August 8, reporting his concern about the losses to his carrier fighter aircraft strength, anxious about the threat to his carriers from further Japanese air attacks, and worried about his ships' fuel levels. It was a much-criticized move, particularly by the Marines holding on at Guadalcanal. As a result of the loss of carrier-based air cover, Rear Adm. Turner decided to withdraw his invasion force ships from Guadalcanal, even though less than half of the supplies and heavy equipment needed by the troops ashore had been unloaded.

As the US transports unloaded on the night of August 8-9 at Guadalcanal, two groups of screening Allied cruisers and destroyers, under the command of British Rear Adm. Crutchley, were surprised and defeated by a Japanese force of seven cruisers and one destroyer from the 8th Fleet based at Rabaul. In the Battle of Savo Island, one Australian and three American cruisers were sunk and one American cruiser and two destroyers were damaged. The Japanese suffered moderate damage to one cruiser that immediately retired to Rabaul without attempting to attack the transports.

The Marines were alone.

Marine division operations officer Lt. Col. Merrill Twining lamented that the 1st Marine Division should be renamed the "1st Maroon Division."[32]

· ✿ ·

---

32   Merrill B. Twinning, Lt. Gen. (Ret.), USMC, *No Bended Knee: The Battle for Guadalcanal.* New York: Presidio, 1996, 88.

SUBMARINE SURPRISE

We had heard rumors of an ever-increasing concentration of Japanese air power and naval strength in the Rabaul and Solomon area. We also received reports of enemy bombing attacks on our ships in Tulagi Harbor and on Lunga Field. Lunga Field came to be called Henderson Field, named after a Marine flyer at Midway. Four of our cruisers were sunk in a night naval engagement off Savo Island. This action was part of the First Defense of Guadalcanal.

One morning in August 1942, I took off on a pre-dawn flight. Just after getting my wheels up and climbing to 500 feet, I saw a submarine sitting with men on deck, on the surface, a very few miles ahead of the fleet. There was a low overhead with heavy dark clouds at 500 feet. I didn't have time or room to make any kind of a dive. With a 500-pound bomb, if you're under 500 feet, you might blow yourself out of the sky.

As I went over the submarine, I dipped my nose and dropped my bomb that exploded alongside. I could see men in the water and the submarine was then sitting tail high out of the water, nose under water. It was in the water in a tail-up position for five or ten minutes. Another plane that took off behind me came over and dropped his bomb. We made four or five runs apiece strafing the sub. We'd fire the twin .50-caliber machine guns in the nose of the SBD and as we turned to make the next run, the rear gunners would shoot the sub with their twin .30s. Amazingly, we never could spare the ammo during training, and I had not fired our .50-caliber guns with live ammo until I fired it at the Japs. When the sub sank underneath the surface, we didn't know what happened to it. However, the Navy gave us credit.

· ❧ ·

A fellow dive-bomber from the so-called Pacific 7 replacements, Lt. Frederick Mears recalled in his *Carrier Combat* written only a couple months after the battle:

One day at that time [August 12, 1942], Bob Gibson and Jerry Richey took off just at dawn and almost immediately surprised a submarine lying on the surface about twenty miles ahead of the carrier. Gibson said it was more accurate to say the submarine surprised him. He almost spun in when he first saw it, he laughed, but managed to make a run on it immediately and drop a 500-pound bomb within feet of it. Richey followed him in and shook the sub by placing his egg within twenty feet of the hull. Thereafter it lay on the surface for five or six minutes in a down-by the-bow attitude while both planes made repeated strafing attacks, firing their fifties forward and their free guns aft. Richey said he saw some Japanese lying on the deck and others struggling in the water. Finally the Japanese prowler settled below the surface, still in a down-by-the-bow attitude but making no apparent headway. Both Gibson and Richey received official commendation for their neat disposal of the raider.[33]

· ✿ ·

"On August 8, Mears was flying a late-afternoon search plane returning after dark. He got lost and was the last to land, having to be given a steer by radio to find Enterprise. *He was waved off for coming in too fast but ignored the wave off and landed on fumes. Hoot was quick to rib him with 'You've got just enough dumb luck to fly over the carrier in the dark without knowing it and catch your hook in a wire.'"[34]*

Lt. Mears did not survive the war.

---

33   Lieutenant Frederick Mears, *Carrier Combat: Battle Action with an American Torpedo Plane Pilot.* Garden City, N.Y.: Doubleday, Doran, 1944.

34   Moore, *Hell's Island*, 210.

Sub-Sinkers
(L to R): E.R. "Hardtack" Anderson, Gibson, Jerry Richey, and
Julian "Toggy" Johnson, August 1942

• ❧ •

Here is the text of the Commendation received by Hoot and Richey.

The following dispatch quoted herewith to be attached to commendation in case of Ensign R.D. Gibson, A-V(N), USNR and Ensign G.S. Richey, A-V(N), USNR:

TACTICAL—12 AUGUST 1942

FROM: C.T.F. 16
TO:C.T.F. 18
INFO:C.T.F. 11

112317

AT 0650 INTERMEDIATE AIR PATROL SIGHTED SUB BELIEVED TO BE TYPE ITEM 121 ON SURFACE APPROX POSIT LAT 17-33 SOUTH LONG 164 EAST ATTACKED BY 2 DIVE BOMBERS WITH 500 LB BOMBS ONE NEAR MISS

AND ONE VERY NEAR MISS ABOUT 15 FEET OVER ON STARBOARD BOW BOTH HIGH ORDER BURSTS

SUB REMAINED ON SURFACE AND WAS HEAVILY STRAFED WITH 50 AND 30 CALIBER MACHINE GUNS.

GRADUALLY SUBMERGED BY BOW WITH NO WAY ON

AT LEAST 4 MEN AFLOAT IN VICINITY

PERSONNEL PRONE ON DECK DURING APPROACH AND ATTACKS

OIL SEEN AROUND SUB IMMEDIATELY AFTER ATTACK BUT SUBSEQUENT SEARCH DID NOT LOCATE SLICK

CONSIDER SUB DESTROYED OR SEVERELY DAMAGED.

UNITED STATES NAVAL CHRONOLOGY WORLD WAR II

AUGUST 1942

7 FRI. Guadalcanal: Marines land on Florida, Tulagi, Gavutu, Tanambogo, and Guadalcanal, Solomon Islands, in the first American land offensive of the war. The 1st Marine Division (Maj. Gen. A. A. Vandergrift) is put ashore by Amphibious Force, South Pacific (Rear Adm. R. K. Turner). The landings are supported by carrier and shore-based aircraft (Rear Adm. L. Noyes and Rear Adm. J. S. McCain). The overall commander is Vice-Adm. R. L. Ghormley, Commander South Pacific, and the officer in tactical command is Vice Adm. F. J. Fletcher.

UNITED STATES NAVAL VESSEL DAMAGED:
•Destroyer *Mugford* (DD-389), by dive-bomber

8 SAT. Marines win control of Tulagi, Gavutu, and Tanambogo, Solomon Islands. An unfinished enemy air strip on Guadalcanal is captured and renamed Henderson Field.

UNITED STATES NAVAL VESSEL SUNK:
• Transport *George F. Elliott* (AP-13), damaged by "suicide" bombers and sunk by US forces

UNITED STATES NAVAL VESSELS DAMAGED:
• Destroyer *Jarvis* (DD-393), by aircraft torpedo
• Transport *Barnett* (AP-11), by suicide bomber

9 SUN. Battle of Savo Island commences in the darkness as a Japanese force of seven cruisers and one destroyer approaches west of Savo Island, Solomon Island, undetected. The enemy sinks four Allied cruisers and damages one other cruiser and two destroyers by torpedo and gunfire before retiring.

UNITED STATES NAVAL VESSELS SUNK:
• Heavy cruisers *Astoria* (CA-34), *Quincy* (CA-39) and *Vincennes* (CA-44) by naval gunfire
• Destroyer *Jarvis* (DD-393) by aircraft attack

UNITED STATES NAVAL VESSELS DAMAGED:
• Heavy cruiser *Chicago* (CA-29) by destroyer torpedo
• Destroyers *Ralph Talbot* (DD-390) and *Patterson* (DD-392) by naval gunfire

CHAPTER FIVE

EASTERN SOLOMONS

Bombing Six, USS Enterprise (CV-6)
"My SBD would sink in 45 seconds."

SBD over Guadalcanal, 1942 (US Navy)

CLASH OF THE CARRIERS

FOLLOWING FLETCHER'S WITHDRAWAL of his carrier task forces, the Japanese sent more reinforcements to Guadalcanal. Admiral Yamamoto put together a very powerful expeditionary force aiming to destroy any American fleet units in the area, and then eliminate Henderson

Field. This force sortied from Truk on August 23. Yamamoto directed a carrier force under Admiral Nagumo from Truk on August 21 to head toward the southern Solomon Islands. Nagumo's force included three carriers and thirty other warships. Yamamoto would send the light carrier *Ryūjō* on a possible bait role ahead of the rest of the fleet, and attack Guadalcanal to draw the attention of the American pilots. The aircraft from the two fleet carriers would then attack the Americans.

Simultaneously, the US carrier task forces approached Guadalcanal to counter the Japanese offensive efforts.

On August 24, the two carrier forces fought. The Japanese had two fleet carriers, *Shōkaku* and *Zuikaku,* and the light carrier *Ryūjō*, with 177 carrier-based aircraft. The American forces had two carriers, the *Saratoga* and the *Enterprise*, and their 176 aircraft. The bait carrier *Ryūjō* was hit by several 1,000-pound bombs, then by an aerial torpedo; she was then abandoned and sank that night. The two Japanese fleet carriers were not attacked. *Enterprise* was attacked and damaged. Both fleets then retreated from the area. The Japanese lost *Ryūjō*, dozens of aircraft, and most of their aircrew; the Americans lost a handful of planes, and *Enterprise* was damaged, needing repair for two months.[35]

· ❖ ·

TWO ARMY HITS

After the invasion of Guadalcanal by our Marines on August 7 and 8, our carrier forces began a game of dodging with the Japanese lasting until August 24, when we clashed head-on again in one of those rugged carrier-versus-carrier slugging matches. This became the first carrier battle following Midway. When two opposing carrier forces meet, both are in for trouble, since it is seldom that one carrier can discover and attack another without being discovered itself. Both usually have almost the same scouting range.

---

35   Hammel, *Guadalcanal: The Carrier Battles*, 46-47.

The US had also established patrol seaplane bases near the action at Guadalcanal. The Japanese, as well, had similar floating bases in the vicinity. Often the two opposing attack groups pass each other in the air on the way to their separate objectives, or the first planes to strike might find themselves flying home, with an enemy air group high in the sky moving in the same direction, as happened to me. It became common practice for both fleets to hit head-on and then to immediately turn tail 180 degrees to avoid any further punishment.

August 24, 1942, the Battle of the Stewart Islands, later called the Battle of the Eastern Solomons, was the third carrier battle—Coral Sea and Midway before it—and the culmination of the First Defense of Guadalcanal. Japan had never let up on bringing reinforcements into Guadalcanal. They sent dribbles of troops landed by submarines on an ongoing basis. However, the next action involved a major thrust by Japan to dislodge the Marines on the island.

I was sent out on a noon search with another pilot, Jigger Lowe. When we got to the end of our search sector, we found the Japanese fleet. The two of us sent in our reports and the *Enterprise* launched her strike group. We climbed to altitude and both dove on a heavy cruiser. I was diving by the books—keeping the sun behind me and facing a pull-out in the direction of my carrier. The target was only fifty feet wide while 600 feet long. Because the ship was turning to avoid my dive at the time to drop the bomb, I found myself going across athwart ships where you don't have much room for error. As a result, I had a near miss on the heavy cruiser *Maya* and so did Jigger Lowe. I swore right then and there never to let the sun or the direction of a safe haven prevent me from hitting the target. From then on I knew that a hit resulted from putting a saddle on the enemy ship and riding that baby down to release.

As we flew back to the *Enterprise*, I could see a Japanese air group from a major carrier flying above me on the same parallel path. We both arrived at the *Enterprise* at the same time. This time I watched the Japanese strike while in my plane circling the fleet. The Japanese scored several bomb hits on *Enterprise*, one of which put a ship's elevator out of commission. Later in the war, *Enterprise* had an elevator blow 400 feet in the air.

· ❦ ·

"Gibson was flying wing on VB-6 exec John Lowe returning from their bombing attack on the cruiser Maya. They reached the **Enterprise** *just as a Japanese attack was underway. Lowe made a low pass over the deck of the* **Enterprise** *so that gunner Gabe Sellers could toss a weighted bean bag message with their contact report. Besides the standard enemy force's composition, course, and speed, it referenced that Gibson and Lowe had made "two Army hits"—near misses—on their targeted warship."*[36]

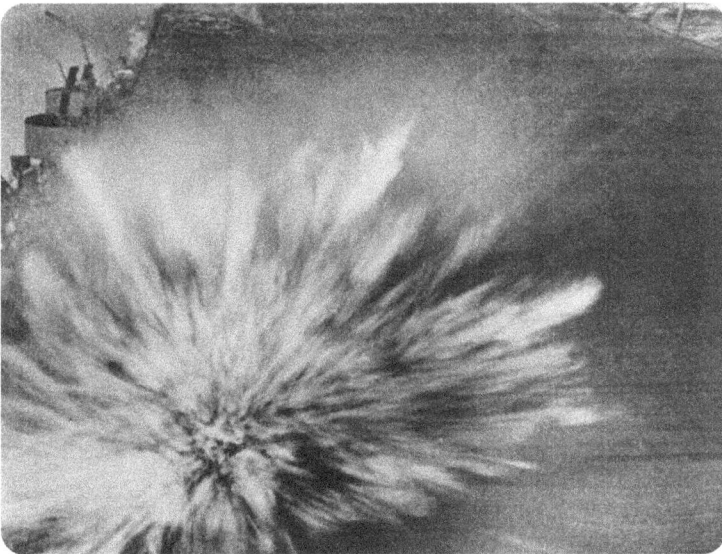

Photo capturing the moment the third of three bombs hit the *Enterprise* flight deck on August 24, 1942, during the Battle of the Eastern Solomons (US Navy)

· ❦ ·

36   Moore, *Hell's Island*, 234.

"We did not get so lucky this time"[37]

Not being able to land during the battle, and finding the nearby *Saratoga* launching instead of retrieving, meant that I ran out of gas within the *Saratoga's* fleet instead of the *Enterprise's* screen of ships. As I struck the ocean, I hit my head on the bombsight and my foot got caught in the railing by the rudder. I pulled my foot out of my shoe and prepared to abandon the plane. I knew the SBD would sink in forty-five seconds. We had a procedure for getting out of the cockpit in case of a forced landing. In this instance, time stopped, and the forty-five seconds allowed seemed like an eternity. Extracting myself was a simple event. There was no hurry at all.

My gunner, Ed "Hardtack" Anderson, was there with the life raft inflated for me to step into. I climbed in without even getting my feet wet. However, that didn't last long as the forty-five seconds sinking time was not up just yet. The waves were tossing the plane back and forth and the tail was slapping the waves in two directions, fore and aft. The plane weighed five tons and the waves were ten feet high. Hardtack, my gunner, and I were in between the tail and the wing. As the waves would knock the tail over and back, staying alive suddenly took on another great aspect. With each wave we had to dive out of the lifeboat to avoid being killed by our former friend, the thrashing SBD.

I was able to land in the ocean near a destroyer of the *Farragut*-class. It was, in fact, the actual *Farragut*. So, I climbed aboard a destroyer out of the drink for the second time in ten weeks. I assumed it was the same destroyer—the USS *Balch*—that rescued me at Midway. As I climbed aboard, I laconically said, "Back again." And the duty officer responded that "We're going to sell you a meal ticket the next time around!" I soon transferred to the *Balch* and they did.

· ❧ ·

---

37   Gunner Ed Anderson, Diary, cited by Moore, *Hell's Island*, 234.

Historian Eric Hammel describes the previous mission and pivotal aircraft battle as:

> Air searchers normally went out 200 miles, flew a cross leg, and then flew back 200 miles to base. However, on August 24, Lt. John Lowe, the Bombing-6 executive officer, and Ens. Bob Gibson, also of Bombing-6, were ordered to fly out fifty miles farther than the usual in the 350—360-degree search sector. Lowe and Gibson flew at 1,000 feet and navigated by dead reckoning.
>
> The two were nearing the tail end of their extended search sector at exactly 3:00 p.m. when they ran into what appeared to be five heavy cruisers and three destroyers bearing 180-degrees and sailing at twenty knots. The position was almost due north of the spot where Lowe and Gibson had launched from *Enterprise*. There appeared to be other ships far to the northwest.[38]
>
> Lowe's radioman immediately transmitted a contact report, but he received no response. Lowe led Gibson up to a higher altitude and tried to send the report again. Still no answer.
>
> Next, the two Dauntlesses circled to the east—up sun and away from the cruiser force—and climbed to 11,000 feet. Lowe had decided to bomb the largest cruiser.
>
> The US Navy dive-bombers pitched over into their dives at 3:10 p.m. As they dived, the cruiser turned her beam to them. As they neared the end of the dive, the cruiser abruptly swung to starboard and skidded around to reverse course. Most of the antiaircraft gunfire was falling away well short of the dive-bombers.
>
> Lowe and Gibson both released their 500-pound bombs at 2,500 feet, glided the rest of the way down to twenty

---

38   These ships were part of Rear Admiral Hiroaki Abe's Vanguard Force, which was serving as the outer screen protecting Admiral Nagumo's Carrier Striking Force from surface attack.

feet off the water and retired to the south at full throttle. On the way down, Lowe's radioman-gunner saw his bomb strike the water about twenty yards off the cruiser's port quarter. Ensign Gibson's bomb hit within twenty-five feet of the cruiser's port bow; its blast sprayed seawater over the cruiser's bow, but did no apparent damage.

Lowe and Gibson returned to the task force on the last of their fuel. Gibson was just turning upwind at 6:10 p.m. to begin his approach on *Saratoga* when his engine died. He ditched dead ahead of cruiser *Minneapolis*, and he and his radioman-gunner climbed out onto one wing. Both airmen were neatly plucked from the water by the destroyer *Farragut*. Lieutenant Lowe landed aboard *Enterprise* at 6:30 without difficulty.[39]

· ✤ ·

Ian Toll sums it up at the end of the day's fighting:

The Battle of the Eastern Solomons was the third carrier battle of the Pacific War. It was a modest tactical victory for the Americans by destroying the Ryujo carrier while saving the *Enterprise* (barely), and by losing only twenty-five aircraft while claiming seventy-five of the enemy. The *Enterprise* had suffered heavy casualties however with two officers and seventy-two seaman killed; six officers and eighty-nine seaman wounded. The first bomb had detonated deep in the ship, and the carnage was appalling. Most of the dead perished quickly, but their bodies had subsequently roasted in the fire. . . . Lack of time and manpower on the stricken ship ruled out committing each body individually to the deep. Under the supervision of the ship's chaplain, a single unidentified sailor was buried with the traditional honors. . . . Some seventy other dead, collected in canvas sacks and

39   Hammel, *Guadalcanal: The Carrier Battles*, 125-126, 210-211.

weighted with spare metal, were dropped from the fantail without ceremony.[40]

Fighting fires in the *Enterprise*'s starboard after 5"/38 gun galley, following a hit by a Japanese bomb during the Battle of the Eastern Solomons on August 24, 1942. (US Naval History and Heritage Command)

* ✿ *

Hornfischer offered a fitting epitaph for the brave sailors buried at sea following the Battle of Eastern Solomons: "In death all sailors have an unmistakable dignity."[41]

---

40   Ian W. Toll, *The Conquering Tide: War in the Pacific Islands, 1942-1944*, New York: Norton, 2015, 83-84 (hereafter *The Conquering Tide*).
41   James D. Hornfischer, *Neptune's Inferno, The US Navy at Guadalcanal*, New York: Bantam, 2011, xviii.

IN WATERS DEEP

In ocean wastes no poppies blow,
No crosses stand in ordered row,
There young hearts sleep...beneath the wave...
The spirited, the good, the brave,
But stars a constant vigil keep,
For them who lie beneath the deep.
'Tis true you cannot kneel in prayer
On certain spot and think. "He's there."
But you can to the ocean go...
See whitecaps marching row on row;
Know one for him will always ride...
In and out... with every tide.
And when your span of life is passed,
He'll meet you at the "Captain's Mast."
And they who mourn on distant shore
For sailors who'll come home no more,
Can dry their tears and pray for these
Who rest beneath the heaving seas...
For stars that shine and winds that blow
And whitecaps marching row on row.
And they can never lonely be
For when they lived... they chose the sea.[42]

---

42   Attributed to Eileen Mahoney, "In Waters Deep," 2001. This touching poem was reportedly written by Ms. Mahoney at age ninety in remembrance of sailors lost in war now serving their eternal patrol beneath the waves. It is perhaps inspired by Lt. Col. John McCrae's heartbreaking World War I poem "In Flanders Fields."

UNITED STATES NAVAL CHRONOLOGY WORLD WAR II

AUGUST 1942

24 MON. Battle of the Eastern Solomons begins and continues into the next day. Naval carrier-based aircraft (Vice Adm. F. J. Fletcher) supported by Marine and Army aircraft turn back major Japanese attempt to recapture Guadalcanal and Tulagi, Solomon Islands.

UNITED STATES NAVAL VESSEL DAMAGED:
- Carrier *Enterprise* (CV6) by dive bomber

JAPANESE NAVAL VESSEL SUNK:
- Carrier *Ryujo*, by carrier-based aircraft

31 MON.

UNITED STATES NAVAL VESSEL DAMAGED:
- Carrier *Saratoga* (CV-3), by submarine torpedo, 260 miles southeast of Guadalcanal, Solomon Islands

• ✦ •

RECOVERY AND NEW CALEDONIA

We transferred from the *Farragut* to the *Balch* and then dropped off onto the same South Seas Islands we had visited before attacking Guadalcanal, the Tongan Islands. At the same airfield in Tonga, we arrived to find that the Air Corps had picked up some new P-40s from Australia. The pilots had no more than ten hours in the plane. One of our hotshot fighter pilots, Machinist Don Runyon, talked to them, teaching them a lot of maneuvers in flying. Runyon was a warrant officer fighter pilot during August 1942 and the Navy's top Wildcat fighter ace during the war, credited with downing eleven Japanese aircraft, including eight during the action off Guadalcanal. One Air Corps pilot named Dave Schilling was transferred to England and became one of the all-time aces. He shot down twenty-two planes and was promoted to colonel by age twenty-five. After his death in a crash in England after the war, the Air Force renamed Smoky Hill Air Base in Kansas after him.

That night there was a conglomeration of Air Corps pilots and a few Navy pilots, as most of them had left the ship to land on Guadalcanal and Efate. I'd say mostly fighter pilots and some SBD pilots from the *Enterprise* were there with the Air Corps guys who were all eager to hear about air tactics that had worked against the Japanese.

There were also some Aussies and New Zealanders. We were delighted to see our old friends in the Air Corps that we had met just before going to Guadalcanal. The only thing to drink, again, was Australian beer, of which they had tremendous quantities. The Aussies were very good imbibers. Their objective was to stay seated at a table all evening without getting up to go to the bathroom. In their estimation, the real test of how much of a man you were was how much beer you could drink and how long you could drink without having to piss. This had never been my nature and I found that I was at that point pretty good at holding the beer, but I couldn't keep it held. So, in spite of their customs, I saw to it that I took care of myself.

About two o'clock in the morning we decided it would be a cute thing to shoot up a little ammunition. A scouting pilot named "Taterhead" Estes and I went outside the Quonset hut and emptied our .45 revolvers into the air, which immediately caused great consternation in the camp. The military police started a frantic search for the culprits, who by this time had dashed across a thirty-yard space, jumped into their army cots and pulled the blankets up over themselves, clothes and all, pretending to be asleep. The military police came through our hut with flashlights trying to find the bastards who had done this dastardly act. By this time, it was 2:30 a.m. At 5:30 a.m. I had to take off to fly inner air patrol for the ship that was coming out of harbor and heading toward Pearl Harbor for repairs.

The airfield was built by the Aussies or New Zealanders. It was a grass field in which they'd interspersed countless holes to allow them to stick poles in the holes to prevent any landings by invading Japanese planes. Any take-off on that grass field was sort of uphill and then downhill to the liking of the Wavy Navy pilots.

But not me. With only three hours sleep, I was completely hung over, still half asleep, having had consumed more heavy beer than I had any right to think about. I had to sit on a hard parachute for six hours before landing on board the carrier at 11:30, hung over, stupid, falling apart, and a physical wreck. However, I was thankful for the pilot's relief tube in the cockpit. Those were the longest six hours of my entire life. Fortunately, I was only twenty-two years old.

Five days after the Big E entered the yard at Pearl, an enemy submarine caught *Wasp* with three big twenty-four-inch torpedoes. They laid her starboard side open and ignited uncontrollable gasoline and ammunition fires that progressively tore her to pieces. My great friend Dick Jaccard, who was the first dive-bomber to hit the carrier *Hiryū* at Midway, was asleep in his bunk after a patrol when one of the enemy warheads obliterated the Officers' Quarters.[43] A dozen pilots that had not been touched in a dozen encounters with the Zeros and the anti-aircraft guns died in their bunks that afternoon of a shot fired from beneath the sea. *Wasp's* crew was forced overboard in a little more than an hour, and by the evening, the most recent US carrier to arrive in the Pacific was a burning derelict that a friendly destroyer had to sink with a second torpedo salvo.

* ❧ *

---

43   Dick Jaccard received the Navy Cross for his actions at Midway. The legacy of Dick Jaccard continued to be honored throughout the war. A Kansas-built B-25 bomber was named the "Jaccard Special" in his honor. Even more significantly, a brand new US Navy destroyer escort, the DE-355, was christened the USS *Jaccard* in his honor.

UNITED STATES NAVAL CHRONOLOGY WORLD WAR II

SEPTEMBER 1942

15 TUE. Carrier task force (Rear Adm. L. Noyes) covering transport of reinforcements from Espiritu Santo, New Hebrides, to Guadalcanal, Solomon Islands, is attacked by two Japanese submarines which sink one aircraft carrier and damage a battleship and a destroyer.

UNITED STATES NAVAL VESSEL SUNK:
- Carrier *Wasp* (CV-7), damaged by submarine torpedo, sunk by US forces

UNITED STATES NAVAL VESSELS DAMAGED:
- Battleship *North Carolina* (BB-55) and Destroyer *O'Brien* (DD-415) damaged by submarine torpedoes

CHAPTER SIX

PEARL HARBOR AND SANTA CRUZ

Bombing Ten, USS Enterprise

His propeller cut off the rear of my plane as if it were slicing salami and ended up within three feet of my cockpit but, fortunately, three inches short of my gunner's cockpit.

Flak attack! USS *Enterprise* in action during the
Battle of the Santa Cruz Islands (Naval History and Heritage Command)

PEARL PERILS

AFTER MY INDISCRETIONS at Tongatapu, I flew back aboard *Enterprise* without incident. The Navy had arranged for us to have rest and recreation at an old mansion on Waikiki Beach just east of the Moana Hotel. The mansion had been owned by Chris Holmes, an heir to the Fleishman Yeast fortune. It was a beautiful place, the entrance coming in from the main drag along Waikiki Beach, and it had an elevator, a beautiful coconut palm grove, and its own beach front. [44]

There were ten or fifteen of us assigned to spend a week there. The officer attached to the property was a man named Soapy Williams from the Williams Aqua shaving fortune in Detroit. Soapy was a big man, friendly, obviously rich, and had a soft touch there in charge of this facility. Later, after the war, Soapy got into politics and was governor of the state of Michigan for many years. In civilian life, he adopted a green and white polka dot bowtie, which was the only tie he ever wore and became his trademark.

Soapy Williams did a good job entertaining us. We had superb food and beautiful bedrooms. Social activities were arranged every night in which the socialites of Hawaii would attend. We met girls who were related to the Castles, Cooks, and the Dillinghams, three of the big five families who had settled Hawaii and owned it, ruling it as kings. Every night after dinner there was a movie or dancing with this social group of Hawaiian girls. It was very exotic, with the smell of gardenias in the air at night and all the other fragrant flowers.

Blackout conditions prevailed, though, and cars couldn't be on the streets after ten o'clock. Any cars driving after dark had to have the headlights painted out with just a small slit about half an inch in height

---

44 Ian W. Toll, *Twilight of the Gods, War in the Western Pacific, 1944-1945*, New York: Norton, 2020, 64-65, 82. The Holmes mansion was the same house used during the Honolulu Conference by President Roosevelt to quarter and meet with his Pacific commanders, Nimitz and MacArthur, in late July 1944, to plan the strategy for the continued war against Japan. Security was a bit heavier and included removing the coconuts on the palm trees that towered overhead lest one should fall and strike the president.

by about an inch and a half in width and the speed limit was five miles per hour. The Navy gave special dispensation to take the girls home after the normal curfew. This was a very idyllic setting, and I was again very happy to be alive.

· �֍ ·

VB-10

Very few pilots had arrived in the Pacific since the day of the Coral Sea battle. The United States had a total of fewer than 300 Navy carrier pilots in the area shortly after the Battle of Midway. I knew about 80 percent of them. By the middle of September, the US had even fewer Navy carrier pilots. By the end of November 1942, this number was reduced to under 100. Meanwhile, the *Saratoga* had been hit again and put out of commission, the *Wasp* was sunk, the *Hornet* was sunk, and the only aircraft carrier in the entire Pacific Ocean was the *Enterprise*. Certainly, at *that* point, I knew every carrier pilot.

Meanwhile, the pilots had either gone back to the States, spent a short period on Guadalcanal and then were sent stateside, or had been killed. Primarily, the flyers whose ships were sunk were sent back to be reassigned. I'd say that practically every pilot who had spent time at Guadalcanal was sent back for rehabilitation. By the end of November of 1942, I was one of the senior pilots in the Pacific—not by rank but as far as actually having combat experience.

In the middle of September I was assigned to VB-10. Group Ten had formed in San Diego and had been stationed at Barber's Point, a new field on the southwest corner of Oahu. I managed to get transportation and was flown out there. Since the Battle of Midway, all of my uniforms and most of my personal possessions were gone. I had little beyond the khakis on my back. I could go to the ship's store and buy khaki shirts and pants on occasion. I probably had one necktie. I managed to get an old pair of hand-me-down shoes from someone, though they didn't quite fit. I cut a hole in one shoe so my toe would stick out.

I arrived as an ensign at Barbers Point on September 21, 1942 and joined Air Group Ten. I was the only pilot who had war experience. Other pilots coming back from Guadalcanal joined the four squadrons. The air group had been transferred intact from the Advanced Carrier Training Group (ACTG) on North Island, San Diego. This was the first time that an entire air group had been trained at ACTG and then transferred to Hawaii to go aboard a carrier, but not the last time.

· ❧ ·

"Lieutenant Commander Frank T. Corbin welcomed Hoot Gibson, who had been through both the Midway and Eastern Solomons carrier battles. However, he had not yet had the chance to bomb a Japanese carrier. 'When will I get that chance?' Gibson wondered. 'It keeps gnawing at me. The sole purpose of being a dive bomber pilot is to help quicken the end of the war by sinking enemy ships.' The frustration was driving him nuts. 'How many more carrier battles will there be while I'm still in the Pacific?'"[45]

· ❧ ·

PROMOTIONS

Lt. (j.g.) Rupert M. Allen reported on board Bombing Ten for duty as air combat intelligence officer on September 28, 1942. When we came aboard *Enterprise*, Rupert was my roommate. There were six pilots senior to me in Bombing Squadron Ten. At that time, I was still an ensign. Two months later, five of the six pilots senior to me were killed, so I became the second-ranking officer in the squadron. The Navy was built around tradition, and the tradition was that you got advanced in rank only through passage of time, with very rigid rules and regulations.

---

45   Moore, *Hell's Island*, 290.

The Army Air Corps had an entirely different concept. A certain rank was attached to the job that you had. If you were twenty-two years of age and you were the second-ranking officer in your squadron, you'd probably be a full colonel—the equivalent of captain in the Navy. In England, in the Air Corps there were many instances of very young twenty-two- and twenty-three-year-old fellows becoming full colonels because of the deaths of senior officers.

I was an executive officer next to the commanding officer of the squadron in charge of leading bombing missions, selecting pilots to go on missions, though I was maybe a j.g. (lieutenant junior grade). This pissed off many Navy pilots. The Marines had a more liberal policy. They would promote faster than the Navy. My Marine friends never held back from rubbing it in.

This was all idle conjecture on my part, as I was only interested in serving in the Navy until the end of the war. It really didn't matter if I received a higher rank. The increase in pay could not be spent at sea. In fact, we played a game of matching half dollars and the loser each time was required to toss his coin into the ocean. I was living like a king on $200 a month. A bullet had not been invented that selected the rank of the individual to drop, so the greatest reward in life then was to stay alive.

* ❧ *

A PACT WITH GOD

One night at Pearl Harbor, before leaving on the next cruise on the *Enterprise*, I walked out from the Officers' Club, and under a full moon made a deal with God: In return for my life, I would be the volunteer under any circumstances. There were many circumstances ahead when I wasn't sure if the pact was still in effect. At those times, I simply never gave up. From the date of the pact onwards I was a leader of pilots, and in a position to name myself as the volunteer pilot for any mission to be assigned.

* ❧ *

DEADLY TRAINING

On September 30, 1942, the air group was making a practice attack, flying south of the coast of Oahu near Barber's Point. We were at about 18,000 feet. It was a beautiful, clear, sunny day, and many ships of the fleet were coming in and out of the harbor. A Navy ship was towing a sled that our group was going to dive on.

All of a sudden, I heard and felt a big boom on the right wing of my plane. As I looked out, I saw the end of my wing and other pieces of airplane parts flying through the air. In the formation a boy from Cleveland named Steve Czarnecki had misjudged and was pulling up into formation underneath the plane beside me. He pulled right up into the propeller of the plane and his plane was cut in two, and half of his head was cut off. A big chunk of his plane, most likely the propeller, sailed through the air like a boomerang and cut off a few feet of my wing.

Strangely, Czarnecki as a reflex action bailed out even though he only had half a head. The other pilot Ralph Goddard and his gunner also managed to bail out and were recovered. Ralph was later killed in the South Pacific.

I decided it was time to bail out myself and I started to climb out on the wing, but the plane seemed to be holding its composure pretty well, so I thought I'd climb back in the cockpit and see what it acted like in a landing attitude. I dropped my landing gear and it worked. I slowed the plane down and dropped the landing flaps, pulling the plane down to just above stalling speed and the plane did not drop off or spin but kept flight altitude. I radioed in the emergency procedure "Mayday," and made a straight descent back to Oahu and to Barber's Point. The field had a long landing strip running east to west. I came from the west over the ocean as the tower cleared the runway and gave me priority. I came in straight-on approach and touched down at the end of the runway at a higher landing speed than normal but had plenty of runway to come to a stop.

Sometime later that day the Navy recovered Czarnecki's body. Since I'd known him in flight training, the skipper of the squadron asked me to go to the morgue at Pearl Harbor to identify the body. I flew to Ford Island the next morning and caught a ride to the morgue. The attendant had bodies in big drawers in a refrigerated area. A drawer was pulled open and there was Czarnecki with his head cut in two, sliced up and down so I could see one eye and one-half of his face. I signed the death papers and stuck the incident into a deep, dark corner of my mind.

In cases where a fellow pilot was killed, one pilot was assigned to ship his personal effects back to his family. On board ship every stateroom had a private safe that was about a foot square and part of the desk where valuables including booze were kept. The first thing a pilot would do was break out the man's booze and drink that, then put everything together in a box and ship it to his parents or the wife back in the States. My single friends and I had a saying, "Other pilots get married, transferred, or *smoked* and it's all the same." Goodbye.

In another incident on a training flight, one of our Wildcat F4Fs, flown by a close friend of mine, crashed into another fighter and chopped his tail off. The pilot was killed—my close friend lived.

On October 11, 1942, Carl Border, one of the pilots senior to me, was taking off from Barber's Point when he crashed at the adjacent Ewa Field in a forced landing with his wheels up. His bomb exploded on impact. This is one of the hazards one faced if you had a belly landing or crash landing, and you had a bomb under your plane—it would likely explode.

This was the second aircraft explosion on take-off or landing that I had seen. The first one had been on Ford Island right after Midway. I was in an administrative office on the second floor as we watched an SBD take off. Construction was going on at the end of the runway and an unseen crane was standing in his line of flight. We saw him crash and as the bomb exploded, we all dove for the deck. Just then I saw the great fear in the face of another pilot. He, no doubt, saw the fear in my face as well. This thing of fear was something you saw every day and almost constantly. You just had to close your mind to it and figure everyone else was going to get killed, but you were not.

I remember the fear that pilots had after the Battle of Midway. We were at Kaneohe at the Officers' Club and several would keep saying, "Well, I'm not going to live through the war, I'm going to be killed." A lot of people talked that way, but I never really believed it would happen to me.

Another pilot was also the type of fellow that you'd pick out as one who was going to be killed. He was a Naval Academy graduate, probably in his late twenties, thin and wiry, sandy complexion, but just didn't quite have the verve that was needed. He was a little too conservative, and you could sense the fear. All it takes is to get in one spot where a pilot doesn't react properly, through fear, and that is the end.

Around this time, some senior-ranking officers decided that Air Group Ten should develop into an all-weather, twenty-four-hour-a-day striking force. But we didn't have the planes or instruments to do it successfully. The junior pilots questioned the reason for practicing what must be done perfectly the first time. That was the Navy's reasoning as applied to parachuting from a plane. The great concept of flying eighty aircraft in formation, in a violent storm, at night had a tragic, short, one-night life.

The apparent idea of this crazy training was to take the entire air group into all the cloudbanks the group could find. That night we lost six planes and four pilots and crews were killed. Among these pilots who died in the fiasco was my best friend at that time, Ralph Goddard. Ralph was a tall, lanky, quiet boy from Minnesota. His father was the superintendent of an Indian reservation stationed in an area that is famous for being the coldest spot in the nation. Ralph had sort of an Abraham-Lincoln manner, so he was very witty, droll, and extremely intelligent. Another wonderful friend who was killed for nothing.

Another senior officer in the squadron to be killed was the executive officer, who was also a Naval Academy graduate. It was obvious to me that he was going to be killed because in one of the battles, we were under a bombing attack and lying on the deck of the ready room. He held his head and moaned that he was going to be killed and he was completely scared to death! At this point I was getting to be accurate many times in judging who was going to live and who wasn't. Of course, I'd had quite a bit of experience by October, and I'd seen dozens of my friends die. However, these sorts of premonitions were not mine alone, as sometimes others would make similar remarks about a person's future.

· 🍁 ·

BACK TO THE FIGHT

By October 16, 1942, major repairs had been completed on the *Enterprise,* and we took off, southward to sea once again. On my first trip to the South Pacific when we crossed the equator, we had no ceremonies because the war was a serious matter and the same way this time there were no ceremonies—I received my diploma from King Neptune but was glad to skip the ceremony.

Enterprise was moving at high speeds near thirty knots, twenty-four hours a day, for a naval engagement that turned out to be the Battle of the Santa Cruz Islands. In that battle we lost a big percentage of our aircraft, and pilots in the air group were either killed, lost at sea, or diverted to land bases. We had been out just a few days before finding action—within ten days our air group's aircraft were practically wiped out. Only three flyable planes were left in Bombing Squadron Ten.

In speeding toward the action, the fleet was traveling with a following wind. That meant that each time takeoff and landing operations were in effect, the fleet was losing double time in its race to engage. As a result, the ship gave absolute minimum air speed across the deck with the result of pilots crashing into the sea during take offs and landings. I experienced a near crash on takeoff with my prop spraying salt water. Pilots were expendable, and any flight could be considered a suicide mission. The Japanese were not alone in dedication to duty.

Events and dates leading up the to the Battle of Santa Cruz on October 26, 1942, sometimes get mixed up because our fleet had just crossed the International Date Line. This time we crossed early in the morning on my birthday. The afternoon before the battle was October 25, when I'd been on a search flight that morning, a four-hour flight, and come back mid-morning. Then at about 5 p.m., the air group was launched to find the Japanese fleet that had been reported sighted.

Tommy Thomas was operating as the air group commander, and I was leading the first section on him, so we were leading the air group. It was not far from the equator and the day was hot as hell. All I had on was a shirt, not a flight jacket. We climbed to 21,000 feet and I've never been so cold in my life, as there was no cockpit heater in an SBD. A little valve you pull out from the windshield was supposed to throw some heat out, but it didn't.

We stayed in formation and flew out 300 miles at this altitude. Then it was starting to get dark, on one of the most remarkable days I've ever seen. The cumulus clouds were built up to 50,000 feet high and were reflecting the setting sun. We had an air group of forty-seven planes in the flight. During the flight I plotted our course, speed, and the time elapsed. We got up to the end of the quadrant in a northwesterly direction and flew a leg of approximately thirty minutes, while the visibility was easily 100-150 miles. It was a spectacular evening.

The sun was setting but we still hadn't spotted the Japanese fleet— down under cloud cover. We reached the end of the cross-leg, and by this time the ocean was dark, but we were up in high sun with clouds below us, though darkness was climbing rapidly toward us. It was one of the most beautiful sights I've ever seen!

As we started back toward the ship, I was numb from cold. It was probably 8:30 pm. We came back when it was totally dark and the only lights we had on were our running lights on top of the wings so the Japanese would have to be on top of us to look down and see any lights. Just at the very last of any light, Tommy gave me an indication to drop our bombs—this was a visual signal—so I passed it on.

As Tommy and I swerved apart to drop our bombs, I looked back for him but couldn't see him. So I made a right-hand turn of about forty degrees to look around and noticed the entire air group following me.

· 🍂 ·

A DARK AND STORMY NIGHT

At age twenty-two and lost at sea on a stormy night, fate had just appointed me the leader of forty-seven carrier aircraft and their crews. I must lead them, in the black of night, back to the carrier and get them safely aboard. I remembered my vow at Pearl Harbor and another power hidden in the dark, rainy sky took hold.

This shook me a little bit and I thought, "Wow, here is an air group following me and I'm just a kid." I thought I'd better make sure, so I made a left-hand turn for 360 degrees and kept looking and finally I could see the lights of forty-seven planes stacked under me making a big broad left-hand turn. Meanwhile, there was no trace of Tommy, the air-group commander. I decided the thing to do was to start letting down and keep my path for where I thought the ship was, just praying that it was there. I reduced throttle and kept my current air speed but started losing altitude and the air group followed suit behind me. By about 9:30 p.m., we did arrive back and found the fleet. Even so, the only light visible was on top of the mast of the two carriers—the *Enterprise* and the *Hornet*. They were in separate fleets but now were cruising beside each other.

On the top mast of the island each carrier made for us alone was a little white running light, barely visible, certainly not visible more than a mile or two. I quickly estimated my gas reserve and figured I had gas left to circle for a while as I knew the fighters would be hard pressed to get in first. Records show that all the fighter planes ditched in the ocean. I made the pass down alongside the ship at 1,000 feet and broke off into the landing circle but immediately climbed back up to a higher altitude and let the planes start landing as they chose. Pilots were running out of gas and landing in the ocean or crashing aboard the deck on occasion as well. As soon as a plane crashed, the crews pushed the wrecks into the ocean to get them out of the way so other planes could come in. Despite that effort, we lost several in the ocean.

Then I could see the other lights of planes landing—some of the planes broke off and went to the other carrier and some went on this one. I didn't know which carrier was which because there was no way of telling if you couldn't see the number because they were identical sister ships.

About the time I figured out I had five gallons of gas left, enough to go around and perhaps take a wave-off. I broke down, got into the landing circle, and came in, got a cut, and landed. I had just landed and had my tail hook disconnected from the landing wire. As I started taxiing forward, I heard the klaxon horns sounding and knew there was a crash coming behind me. It was "Tiny" Carroom, who had disobeyed the landing signal to take a wave-off because he was too close on my tail. He took the cut regardless and was landing right beside me. His propeller cut off the rear of my plane as if it were slicing salami and ended up within three feet of my cockpit, but, fortunately, three inches short of my gunner's cockpit. Having lost part of my right wing a couple of weeks before to another wingman's negligence, I was left feeling that I was getting chopped all around.

Both planes were tossed overboard, but I was still fortunate to be alive onboard ship instead of in the ocean. I supposed most of the men got picked up—I don't know. I do know the next day, as I watched the battle from the flight deck, it appeared that our fleet went off and left many planes and pilots floating around in the water without any hope of recovery. Screening ships may have been behind to pick up the pilots. I certainly hope so. Most of my squadron survived, including Tommy.

· ❧ ·

THE BATTLE OF SANTA CRUZ

Yamamoto wanted revenge for Midway. He sent Adm. Nagumo's three-carrier strike force and a vanguard battleship force south to lure the elusive American carriers to their destruction and to support the Japanese 17th Army offensive to take back Guadalcanal.

In late October, Japanese aircraft carriers and other large warships moved into a position near the southern Solomon Islands. From this location, the Japanese naval forces hoped to engage and decisively defeat any US naval forces, especially any carrier forces that responded to Japan's renewed ground offensive on Guadalcanal. Allied naval carrier forces in the area, now under the overall command of Vice Adm. Halsey, also hoped to meet the Japanese naval forces in battle. The two opposing carrier forces confronted each other on the morning of October 26, in what became known as the Battle of the Santa Cruz Islands.

The carrier Hornet was torpedoed and fatally damaged by a Japanese carrier. After an exchange of carrier air attacks, Allied surface ships were forced to retreat from the battle area with the loss of the Hornet and with the Enterprise again heavily damaged. The participating Japanese carrier forces, however, also retired because of high aircraft and aircrew losses and significant damage to two carriers. Although a tactical victory for the Japanese in terms of ships sunk and damaged, the loss by the Japanese of many irreplaceable, veteran aircrews provided a long-term strategic advantage for the Allies, whose aircrew losses in the battle were relatively low. The Japanese carriers played no further significant role in the campaign.[46]

· ❧ ·

---

46   Morison, *The Struggle for Guadalcanal*, 207-224; Richard B. Frank, *Guadalcanal: The Definitive Account of the Landmark Battle*, New York: Random House, 1990, 379-403.

THE BULL IS BACK![47]

Just before midnight on October 24, as his marines ashore were battling the Japanese assault, Halsey radioed his principal naval commanders, Kincaid and Lee, with a galvanizing message that would echo through the passageways and compartments of every ship in the South Pacific Force. The four syllables, bereft of any operational specificity or doctrinal nuance and apropos of no particular target, placed a clean vector through everyone's mind that ordered and oriented their next moves.[48]

"STRIKE—REPEAT, STRIKE."

· ❋ ·

INCOMING!

The next morning, since I had flown late, the reserve pilots took off on the early morning flights and I slept in. At about ten o'clock the Japanese aircraft carriers sent strike groups coming over the *Enterprise* and the *Hornet* in several waves.

Each fleet had twelve to fifteen ships, but enemy aircraft were out to get only the two carriers. There were three Japanese carriers, so they had a potential of 200 planes for the strikes. They were split pretty much fifty-fifty above the *Enterprise* and the *Hornet*. The first wave came in while I was in the ready room, where the policy was to hit the deck to save our lives. On occasions like this, the ship would go into violent gyrations. We had a huge fifty-cup coffee urn sitting on a table, which tipped over, sending us all swimming around in hot coffee.

Jack Dufficy, a highly likeable Special Services officer attached to

---

47   Vice Adm. "Bull" Halsey had just replaced Vice Adm. Ghormley as commander, South Pacific Forces. Rear Adm. Thomas Kinkaid led the US two-carrier task force (TF 61) from the *Enterprise* and Rear Adm. Willis Lee led the battleship task force (TF 64) from the *Washington*.
48   Hornfischer, *Neptune's Inferno*, 222.

VB-10, was an attorney from Long Island. He was an older man in his mid-thirties and had a great sense of humor. Short and pudgy and with a big wide smile, Jack remarked, "I had to get six guys' permission to get off the deck," meaning he was the quickest man to hit the deck and others had piled on him while he was spread-eagled there.

* * *

FLOOR FOR ONE PLEASE!

"Someone with a sense of humor, and less regard for the accuracy of Japanese bombing, took a moment to draw an outline around the prostrate officer," said Hal Buell. In block letters, the chalk outline drawing was labeled RESERVED FOR LT. DUFFICY.[49]

* * *

BOMB DODGER

I heard something strange to me and knew the ship was hit.

Remember, I had been aboard *Yorktown* when it took three bombs and three torpedoes. In fact, as an experienced bomb dodger, I was able to beat Dufficy to the deck every time. This strange happening was my introduction to a tandem bomb dropped by the Japanese. The first tandem bomb went below to officers' country and the top bomb exploded almost simultaneously above it.

Meanwhile the other fleet of aircraft was hitting the *Hornet* very successfully. The *Hornet* was in much worse condition than the *Enterprise.* I thought, "Thank God, that the unknown ship I landed on last night was my ship, instead of the *Hornet.*"

The ready room filled up with smoke again and I said, "To hell

---

49   Moore, *Hell's Island,* 336, citing Harold L. Buell's *Dauntless Helldivers: A Dive-Bomber Pilot's Epic Story of the Carrier Battles.* New York: Orion, 1991, 143.

with this, I'm going up on the flight deck." There I watched the next wave of planes attack our ship. At the same time, our strike aircraft were coming back to land on the ship and couldn't get aboard, as we were on fire after the enemy planes had retreated. We had been told that something like twenty submarine reports had been made in the area, and the admiral and captain of the ship were very concerned about being hit by subs. They had this to contend with, plus the violent air action going on at the same time and I thought, "Why in the hell am I once again stuck aboard ship when I should be bombing a carrier?"

I saw a TBF torpedo plane (Dick Batten was later identified as the pilot) crash into the water behind the carrier alongside a destroyer [USS *Porter*]. The destroyer slowed down, reached over, and pulled the pilot and crewmen out of the water, but hadn't got back underway again when a torpedo from a sub hit the destroyer and exploded. The destroyer broke in half and sank almost immediately. So, Batten and his crew were back in the drink within minutes of rescue. They were eventually recovered and I would often tease Batten about the feckless adventure.

· ✤ ·

Remarkably, Batten's adventure was more feckless than thought at the time. In a bizarre twist, it is now believed that the *Porter* was not sunk by a torpedo from a Japanese sub, but from Batten's own TBF Avenger torpedo plane instead! Batten still had not been able to dump his torpedo when he was waved off from landing on the *Enterprise*. When Batten ditched his plane, the impact released the torpedo that was jammed underneath which went on a circular run—which torpedoes are apt to do—and came back to hit and sink the destroyer which had stopped to pull Batten out of the drink. Some reward. [50]

· ✤ ·

50   Cox, *Morning Star, Midnight Sun: The Early Guadalcanal-Solomons Campaign of World War II*, August – October 1942. Oxford: Osprey, 2018, 367.

Something inside of me still refuses to research whether the Navy made a real attempt to recover many pilots, such as Batten, that landed in the ocean that day and appeared to be abandoned by the fleet. I hope the ships did return to the search area, but I am fearful of the answer. To my knowledge, no air searches were made.

• ✿ •

SOUTHERN SKEDADDLE II

The damage from the Japanese bombing this day was almost identical to that made by the bomb that hit the *Enterprise* on August 24 in the Battle of the Eastern Solomons. Both bombs hit an area with an ammunition elevator—which is like a dumbwaiter. That elevator shaft sucked fire right down into the munitions locker. You can guess the results. And again, the damage was extensive. Once it temporarily recovered from the air attack, the fleet turned and headed due south, full speed ahead.

At the same time our fleet turned south, the Japanese fleet did a 180 and turned back north—both fleets scared to death that the other fleet was closing in on them. The *Hornet* was sunk, and the *Hornet's* planes were landing on the *Enterprise*. The US had lost many planes within a twenty-four-hour period. Starting with over 160 airplanes the day before, we probably had fifty left. A number of pilots had been lost as well.

That evening after watching all the action, a further grisly undertaking took place in the wardroom as the pilots ate dinner. Sickbay had been wiped out and floodlights had been brought into the wardroom to provide light for operating on the wounded. One half of the tables were used for operating tables, the other half were being used for serving and eating dinner. Water on the deck from fighting fires was ankle deep as we stood in line to get our food trays. The strong smell of chloroform, antiseptics, and death permeated the air from the multiple operations going on at a time.

Battle of Santa Cruz: October 26, 1942. The dive bomber attack on the *Enterprise*, as seen from the USS *Portland*. The carrier is listing some fifteen degrees, but damage control can still be seen on the flight deck. (US Navy)

The next day we had further scares from reports of sightings of the *Enterprise* by Japanese search planes. Bombing Ten had few flyable planes but even they had some damage. I was out with the crews putting adhesive tape on the control surfaces of the ailerons and stabilizers. Our pilots were fighting each other to get to take off from the carrier because no one wanted to be on board when the next Japanese bombing attack occurred. Only three Bombing Ten pilots could escape the target ship, *Enterprise*, at any one time. Fortunately, another attack did not develop.

· ❧ ·

AND THEN THERE WAS ONE

The Battle of the Santa Cruz Islands was the fourth carrier battle of the war and the last until the Battle of the Philippine Sea in 1944. Although the contest would go into the book as a tactical victory for the Japanese, it was a strategic victory for the Americans. The destruction of the *Hornet* left the Allies with just one carrier in the theater—the wounded *Enterprise*. In exchange, the Americans had damaged two Japanese carriers, but destroyed neither. Plane losses were roughly comparable—eighty-one for the Americans, ninety-nine for the Japanese. But the Americans recovered many of their downed aviators. They lost only twenty-six airmen, while the Japanese lost 148, and among the latter's dead were twenty-three squadron or section leaders, all prized veteran flyers who could not be easily replaced.[51]

· ❧ ·

ROYAL [HAWAIIAN] REPRIMAND

On October 27, our captain stood in front of the pilots in the ready room and said, "I have a telegram from Pearl Harbor. It was sent by the shore patrol headquarters in Hawaii and forwarded through Admiral Nimitz. It lists three pages of infractions of naval regulations that some pilots had committed the last night in Pearl Harbor." He said, "I'm going to read this to you." It called for strong disciplinary action against the jackasses involved, including me, and then he looked at me, laughed, and said, "Consider that you have been severely punished."

What had happened was that a few pilot friends and I were involved in an altercation with the shore patrol—yet only a very few days later, many of the guys were dead and the ship was badly damaged and heading for New Caledonia to be repaired. What had happened the night before we left Pearl Harbor was a bunch of the boys were in the Royal Hawaiian and drinking. We had a little game we played—though it was blackout. All halls were dimly lit, and the windows in the rooms were blacked out. There were very few women around, but they were sorely missed. We would get two rooms across the hall from each other, take the sheets

---

51   Toll, *The Conquering Tide*, 153-154.

off the beds and tie them together to make a rope stretching across the hallway. Anytime a man came down the hall with a girl, we would yank the sheets to trip them and then we would grab the girl. This was all in fun, and only once did I see a fist hit a chin. This kind of action was alleged in later years and brought great sorrow to the Tailhook Association.

We played this game until several got tired and went to bed. Then a few of us decided to go outside and play more games. So, we took our whiskey bottles and went out to Kalakaula Avenue, the main drag on Waikiki. We were roaming up and down in front of the hotel whooping and hollering and raising hell, drinking. The shore patrol came up and we didn't have any insignias on or ties or hats. We were supposed to wear gas masks, hat, tie, jacket, and insignia, and carry a .45 revolver. We weren't supposed to be on the streets; we were expected to be in bed, sober, and sensible.

Instead, we told the shore patrol to go to hell and walked off and left them. We went back to the hotel and went to bed. Of course, they had gotten each of our names. That was our battle with the shore patrol.

* ❋ *

NEW CALENDONIA

The ship was constantly changing course and running at top speed until October 30 when we reached port in New Caledonia. The ship would immediately start repairs and the squadron was looking for replacement aircraft and pilots to appear. None of the replacements came in large numbers; it was usually a dribble. A normal squadron might have twenty-one to twenty-five pilots and eighteen to twenty-one planes. We had between fifteen to twenty pilots with eighteen planes. And the new pilots were all green, just as we had been. We were transferred from the ship in Nouméa. We didn't fly ashore as usual because of the lack of planes and the fact that the three planes left were kept aboard to be repaired.

New Caledonia was a friendly Free French island off the coast of Australia, and the terrain was reminiscent of California. Beautiful rolling hills and mountains appeared as those on our West Coast. The Navy never put into Australia because of fear that MacArthur would take our ships. No one in the Navy liked MacArthur, therefore New Caledonia was the safe harbor instead of some Australian port.

We went ashore on a liberty boat from the *Enterprise* that was anchored out in the harbor. The minute we got into harbor, construction workers came aboard and started repairing damages. One of the bomb hits in August had landed just aft of the island structure and the ship caught on fire. The next plane in the dive had a near-miss along the starboard midship, so the geyser of water that came up extinguished the fire! The ship had also suffered extensive damage along the starboard waterline where there was a rip in the seam that was probably fifty feet long and a foot wide, requiring constant pumping all the way from Santa Cruz to New Caledonia. The construction battalion worked twenty-four hours a day.

The pilots went ashore and got transportation to go to an island airstrip about forty miles up the island called Tontuta. The airstrip was going to be quite an active airfield. It had Marston matting covering the runway. The technology used metal strips with holes punched in them that would easily lay on the ground. It was easy to work with and quickly provided a semi-permanent dependable landing area.

It was a great pleasure to get into Nouméa and see the culture of the Free French who were living there and still allied with America. We marveled at the sidewalk urinals—I'd never seen that before. Beautiful vegetation, flowers, hills, grass, and trees were all familiar, just as were parts of New Guinea that I was in later in the war, which also had somewhat the same appearance as Southern California. The hills were brown, eucalyptus trees were green, the shoreline along the ocean was beautiful and rugged, and the hills and mountains came up to the ocean joined by plains and beautiful sandy beaches. A lot of charm was evident in the town of Nouméa. It had perhaps 5,000 in population, maybe 10,000. There was a lot of activity. Other US carriers, including the *Wasp*, had come into harbor earlier, but now there was only one carrier left in the South Pacific fleet and that was the *Enterprise*. The Navy wanted to get *Enterprise* back into action, and that was reflected in the feverish activity around us in port.

• 🍁 •

FAMOUS FOLKS

Turn the clock back to my boarding the *Enterprise* in October outbound from Hawaii. Upon finding my quarters, I soon found my new roommate Rupert Allen. He was an AVS officer, and the letters stood for aviation specialist. Rupert had been commissioned at Quonset Point, Rhode Island, in a sped-up program. The Navy nicknamed such officers *Ninety-Day Wonders*. The officers coming out of the program were to handle administrative details for carrier squadrons in order to take the paperwork burdens from the pilots. These people were highly selected for their maturity and levels of education. Rupert, for example, was assigned to duty for Bombing Ten as the air intelligence officer with responsibilities of debriefing each pilot after actions, making reports for the Navy, and for maintaining an active log of all the squadron's activities. Rupert was a graduate of a major private university, after which he entered Oxford for graduate studies.

After the war, Rupert was considered the dean of old public relations and lived in Beverly Hills representing and personally assisting the most famous actors and actresses in the world. For example, Marilyn Monroe was a client, and he was called very soon after Monroe was found dead in 1962. Rupert shared a home with movie producer Frank McCarthy, who served as a brigadier general in Europe during the war under General Patton. He later produced the movie *Patton*.

The other new friend I discovered on this cruise sat across the dining table from me on occasion. He was extremely polite, but further distinguished himself by his curious mind. He was constantly barraging me about current affairs. How did I see the eventual outcome of Stalingrad? What did I think of the island-hopping concept for bypassing islands with heavy concentrations of Japanese? On and on. Eventually, after such an interrogation, I asked him his name. He answered, "Field, Marshall Field," one of the ship's gunnery officers. I thought, boy the military sure reduces each one down to a common denominator. Put the same clothes on everyone and they are all the same. Put any one person in front of a bullet, and they die the same as anyone else.

Marshall's gun position was equipped with forty-millimeter *pom-poms*, an anti-aircraft battery on the hull deck, called the *weather deck*, just under and out front of the forward end of the flight deck. It was built on a platform eight or more feet above the hull deck. During the enemy air attacks in the Battle of Santa Cruz, one bomb angled through the flight deck and exploded in the ocean near his gun mount. The upward blast blew Marshall out of the mount and down to the deck, barely missing sending his body into the sea. Immediately Marshall climbed to his firing position and kept the quads of his guns firing on other Japanese planes. Here again is demonstrated the common equalizer effect of a uniform bearing no name, other than that of the Average American.

I asked Marshall one day across the table if he would like to take a flight with me, and I would show him the effects of a dive from high altitude. He said he would like to do so, and he showed up one day at the field where the pilots were stationed. I forget which island, but I strapped him into a chute and off we went. He survived. Marshall was number IV in his family. Number I started the Chicago retail empire, number II had died, and number III was referred to as "Old Field." He was the owner of the *Chicago Sun-Times* that ran a series of articles about the war and the *Enterprise*, as written by "an officer from the *Enterprise*." The articles were, of course, written by IV, Marshall. After the war, I worked for Marshall for six years. What a guy! Marshall never forgot me, nor did the Navy.

· ❀ ·

UNITED STATES NAVAL CHRONOLOGY WORLD WAR II

OCTOBER 1942

18 SUN. Vice Adm. W. F. Halsey relieves Vice Adm. R. L. Ghormley as Commander, South Pacific Area and South Pacific Force.

26 MON. **Battle of Santa Cruz Islands** is joined as carrier task forces [Rear Adm. T. C. Kinkaid and Rear Adm. G. D. Murray] close with a numerically-superior Japanese force; heavy damage is inflicted on United States forces but immediate Japanese movement toward Guadalcanal, Solomon Islands, is checked.

Battle of Henderson Field, Guadalcanal, Solomon Islands, ends as Marines repulse Japanese land and air attacks.

UNITED STATES NAVAL VESSELS DAMAGED/SUNK:
- Carrier *Enterprise* [CV-6] by dive bomber
- Carrier *Hornet* [CV-8] by air attack
- Battleship *South Dakota* [BB-57] by dive bomber
- Light cruiser *San Juan* [CL-54], by dive bomber
- Destroyer *Porter* [DD-356] by submarine torpedo
- Destroyer *Smith* [DD-378] by suicide bomber
- Destroyer *Hughes* [DD-410] by collision

27 TUE.

UNITED STATES NAVAL VESSEL SUNK:
- Carrier *Hornet* [CV-8] by dive and torpedo bombers, and destroyer torpedoes

UNITED STATES NAVAL VESSELS DAMAGED:
- Battleship *South Dakota* [BB-57] and Destroyer *Mahan* [DD-363] by collision

CHAPTER SEVEN

NAVAL BATTLE OF GUADALCANAL: THE THIRD DEFENSE

Bombing Ten, USS Enterprise
"Here Goes"

Bombing Squadron Ten—USS *Enterprise*; Hoot Gibson is standing fifth from left. (Left to right are (first row) Wiggins, Buell, Frissel, Robinson, Stevens, Dufficy, Leonard, Welch, McGraw, and Thomas; (back row) Wakeham, Griffith, Hoogerwerf, Goddard, Gibson, Halloran, Buchanan, Nelson, Allen, West, and Carroum. (US Navy, NA 80-G-30069)

DERAILING THE TOKYO EXPRESS

THE TOKYO EXPRESS was the name coined by Allied forces for the Japanese night convoys delivering personnel, supplies, and equipment to Japanese forces operating in the Solomon Islands. The convoy of fast warships—mainly destroyers—and later submarines, used speed to deliver the personnel or supplies to the desired location and return to the originating base all within one night so Allied aircraft could not intercept them by day. The Japanese called the night resupply missions *Rat Transportation*, because they took place at night.[52]

* ❋ *

ENTERPRISE VERSUS JAPAN

The *Enterprise* was a survivor. She had taken two direct bomb hits and two near misses while evading nine torpedoes and landed two carriers' worth of returning aircraft at the Battle of Santa Cruz. But she was wounded. Her flight deck elevators were jammed, and she had an open seam of fifty feet in her side plating. Her main turbine bearing was damaged, along with three fuel tanks that had ruptured. Among other critical damage, she was down four feet at the bow. Repairs were estimated to take three weeks just to get her modestly operational. She was back at sea in just eleven days due to a herculean effort of Seabees and construction crews. Now she had a chance to strike back at the Japanese and set things straight for Santa Cruz. Her men hung a message of defiance: *Enterprise* versus Japan.[53]

On November 13, 1942, Vice Adm. Halsey directed Rear Adm. Kincaid, carrier task force commander, to release his battleships *South Dakota* and *Washington* to enter the naval fight at Guadalcanal. He also ordered the *Enterprise* north from Nouméa toward Guadalcanal. "She carried with her a crew of eighty-five repair technicians aboard still working

---

52   Frank, *Guadalcanal*, 268.
53   Cox, *Blazing Star, Setting Sun*, 141-143.

to fix the damaged forward elevator. She also trailed an oil slick."[54]

Wounded *Enterprise* at Nouméa, November 10, 1942
(US Navy Archives, NA 80-G-30547)

· ✳ ·

THE DECISIVE MÊLÉE

"This was the tightest spot that I was
ever in during the entire war."

—Vice Adm. William "Bull" Halsey

The Japanese planned to try again to retake the airfield in November 1942, but further reinforcements were needed before the operation could proceed. The Japanese Army commanders requested assistance from Yamamoto to deliver the needed reinforcements to the island and to support the next offensive.

In November, both navies ferried convoys of reinforcements to Guadalcanal. The Americans arrived on November 12, unloading 5,500 men without incident. Six hundred miles away, 7,000 Imperial soldiers boarded Japanese transports, while an advance fleet of destroyers and

---

54   Hornfischer, *Neptune's Inferno*, 336.

cruisers headed out to shell Henderson Field.

Allied intelligence learned that the Japanese were preparing again to try to retake Henderson Field. Although severely outgunned, American Task Force 67 quickly escorted their transports to safety, then bravely turned around to intercept the enemy. As darkness fell on the night of November 12, the opposing ships confronted each other in furious point-blank fire. In the pitch darkness the two warship forces intermingled before opening fire at unusually close quarters. Shells slammed one after another, sometimes streaking over the bow of one ship only to blast the superstructure of another. In the resulting mêlée, Japanese warships sank or severely damaged all but one cruiser and one destroyer in the American task force lead by Rear Admirals Callaghan and Scott; both Callaghan and Scott were killed. It was a brutal engagement for both sides, but it was clearly won by the Japanese. Five American and three Japanese ships went down, along with more than 2,000 Japanese soldiers.

Yamamoto again dispatched his fast cruisers to Guadalcanal, and in the early hours of November 14, they successfully shelled Henderson Field. American fighter planes scrambled to get airborne and score hits, as did airplanes launched from the *Enterprise*.

As the Japanese reinforcement convoy set sail, Admiral Halsey ordered his battleships to Savo Island. Fourteen Japanese warships were still approaching Savo Island and, as the sun went down on November 13, the American battleships were ready. Once again, the night fighting was a terrifying cacophony of guns and bombs. The waters were crowded with warships and transports, and the pilots from Henderson and *Enterprise* attacked them unopposed. The American planes picked their targets and bombed away, sinking six transports and turning away three more. By dawn, eight American ships and twenty-three Japanese vessels had sunk to the bottom of Iron Bottom Sound.

Because of the failure to deliver most of the troops and supplies, the Japanese were forced to cancel their planned November offensive on Henderson Field, making the battle a significant strategic victory for the Allies, and marking the beginning of the end of Japanese attempts to retake Henderson Field. This was the decisive moment. The Japanese command realized it could not dislodge the Americans from Hell's Island.[55]

· ❀ ·

MY STORY

As I recount the stories below, I want to spell out my long, enduring friendship with Tommy Thomas up until his death, and my love for the Navy. I make remarks, not about the person or the service, but of the essential nature of the world, and life, that cause happenings and procedures to gain form automatically, with little influence from any one person. Procedures within a service exist because they work, even though the ideal observer might tell us that certain modifications would give better results. Even so, I understand tradition and respect it. Sometimes an individual suffers harm from a tradition that is meant to help. Tommy had his devils in mind to live with, although he may have been mainly the wrong person at the wrong place at the wrong time. Please read this chapter in this context.

After two tragic events of the Guadalcanal strike and the horrific night, weather grope, Tommy became withdrawn, and I was left with more responsibilities in the daily operations of the squadron. Senior members of other squadrons approached me in support. I remembered the pact with God I had made at the Pearl O'Club and let it go at that. I had agreed to volunteer for any assignment in return for my life. Sometimes a belly full of whiskey and a full moon works miracles.

· ❀ ·

55   Douglas L. Keeney and William S. Butler, *This is Guadalcanal: The Original Combat Photography*, New York: William Morrow, 1998, 114; Frank, *Guadalcanal*, 462-492; Hammel, *Guadalcanal: Decision at Sea: The Naval Battle of Guadalcanal, November 13-15,1942*. New York: Crown, 1988, 345-349, 363-368,385-398, 430-438.

Having arrived at Tontuta Airfield in New Caledonia, we proceeded to our tent city near the airfield. We counted Jack Dufficy, Rupert Allen, Tommy Thomas, Ed Stevens, and me, all in our squadron at that time who were alive and available. The squadron was joined by a few replacement pilots, and we received new replacement aircraft.

Part of the procedures for getting a new plane ready to fly involved calibrating the compass located in the cockpit. It is possible to deviate a compass by the installation of magnetic metals, such as armor plating around the pilot's seat. Each and every plane had its own peculiarities that needed to be addressed. Since our lives depended upon dead-reckoning navigation, the corrections for compass calibration were printed on a card affixed to the compass near the windshield. The process involved hoisting the tail of the plane to put the plane in a flying attitude over a painted compass on a concrete slab, Then, we revved up the engine to full speed, pivoted the plane around over the painted compass, and recorded the differences in compass readings and the true coordinates. This *had* to be done by the pilots, as their lives that were at stake if they did not.

All guns were checked, then ammunition, bombsites, engines, controls, etc. Then we started training the new pilots. Again, every day was flight day—either you were in action or in training—the disciplines that accounts for the great record the Navy had. Training never ceased. We flew every day, and that meant four to eight hours a day so that no one got rusty.

But we had lots of fun on the island, too. There was deer hunting. Several fellows shot deer and we had venison at the mess. The toilet was a forty-hole sensation, called a *chick sale* for some forgotten reason. Modesty flew out the window. Yet, one could go there in the morning to hear all the gossip about what had happened in the other squadrons the night before.

Naturally, we had an officers' club set up—a tent with some booze. There was a French plantation down the road where we'd go to buy dinner and French wine. One night coming home, a deer walked in front of us and was killed. It too, ended up on our dinner plates. One time at the French planter's house, I got into a craps game with a group of French soldiers. Every time I tossed in a twenty-dollar bill, the French would grab it and toss in a fist full of francs. The next morning, I awakened to find several thousand francs in my pockets instead of American money. Sadly, I never converted them back into US currency.

This life was camping out and living in nature, and this period, along with other personal experiences throughout the war satisfied any desire I might have had for camping thereafter. I prefer the Ritz Carlton. In the mornings at our tent city, you'd shave with cold water—you'd go over to a tank, turn a spigot, fill a cup, pour a little in your shaving cream, shave without a mirror but by feel, brush your teeth over the ground, go to the chick sale, and then go down to the squadron and get the planes ready to get back into action.

We were there several days when we were informed that the next morning we were taking off to land aboard the ship, then going to sea and heading back to Guadalcanal. My radioman-gunner was Clifford E. Schindele, ARM2/c, a product of North Dakota where people learn to be self-reliant in an extreme environment. He was a serious and smart friend and companion, and one to be relied upon when things got tough, which things did—more than once. I have often thought about asking him what was going through his mind, then and now, when our lives were hanging on a very thin thread.

· ❧ ·

"Dive on [heavy] Cruiser. Left Ship Burning. Continuing to Cactus."[56]

The *Enterprise* got under way in the early morning of November 11, 1942 and came back up to a position about 200 miles south of New Georgia Island, northwest of the west tip of Guadalcanal. We were 250 miles away from Henderson Field when the action began on November 14.

---

56   ARM2 Cliff Schindele action report transmitted at 9:44 a.m. November 14, 1942.

On November 13 the *Enterprise* sent a half dozen TBFs to Guadalcanal at Henderson Field, code-named *cactus*. That morning our troops had been alerted that the Japanese were planning a strong counteroffensive to land an estimated 13,000 troops on Guadalcanal. Their intent was to concentrate enough strength to run the Marines and the Army off and to recapture Guadalcanal. They at first thought the Americans would not make a strong fight to hold it, but they were proven wrong.

On the early morning of November 14, I was assigned a search sector that went due north from our fleet 250 miles. Leading a two-airplane search, I had Ensign Richard Buchanan on my wing. When we got to the end of the search at about 7:30 am, we discovered a Japanese fleet of cruisers and destroyers.

**Take Off! Rear Gunner's photo of launch off the Big E.
Note vertical tail of the aircraft in lower right. (US Navy)**

We circled the Japanese fleet while climbing to an altitude of 18,000 feet, flying in and out of clouds to take advantage of cover to avoid Zeros and the anti-aircraft fire the enemy was firing. The contact reports sent the composition of the fleet, its direction, and speed of its action. Based upon my reports, the admiral launched the attack group from the carrier, and they homed in on my contact reports. My skipper, Tommy Thomas, was flying in the air group, proceeding according to the contact reports. This exemplified the perfect coordination for finding the enemy and at the same time delivering the attack.

Cliff was sending reports from my notes on the long-range high-frequency transmitter, and I was repeating each message by voice. The clothesline was getting hot from a real workout going back and forth from cockpit to cockpit. Each message reflected our current assessments of the Japanese fleet. By coincidence, Doan Carmody was reporting contact with another Japanese fleet in the search sector next to mine simultaneously with my reports. John Crommelin said, "This is the best contact report made in the war." John perhaps didn't know that there were two of us searching and reporting on separate enemy fleets at the same time.

Buchanan and I dove on the ship about 9:00 a.m. and later learned that the target was the *Kinugasa*, a heavy cruiser with a long history of action during the War. During the dive I thought, *It's entirely possible that this is the same ship I dove on three months ago.* So, here was a chance to rectify a near miss in August when I had gotten trapped on a bomb run, ending up dropping athwart ship. Later, I learned that the August ship was the heavy cruiser, *Maya.* Athwart ship approach gives one less than a fifty-foot margin of error each way. This time I locked on the target, always facing stern to bow, just as though I were once again taking a shot with a rifle against a flying squirrel. I swore I was going to hit this squirrel and rode on the ship's back as though in a saddle.

The advantage of dive bombing over horizontal bombing on a moving target can best be described this way. High results, as proven by my hits on moving ships, can be obtained by diving aft to fore, staying locked on the target, keeping the dive angle less than 70 percent, keeping the ball in the needle-ball instrument *in its cage* to maintain a *non-skid* dive throughout, and releasing the bomb below 2,000 feet. With this dive configuration, the airplane simulates a rifle, and the heavy bomb travels the same trajectory as a rifle bullet. Bomb release to impact is less than four seconds and reaches the target the same as if the plane dove straight into the ship. This resulted in a high-hit ratio prior to the development of smart bombs.

At this point in the war, the Navy's dive bombers were experiencing a hit ratio of 40 percent, up from 30 percent earlier on. Mathematically, the odds of hitting a moving ship at thirty knots by horizontal bombing was less than 1 percent. This low rate was continuously verified throughout the war. Simply put, while bombs are falling from altitude, a ship traveling at thirty knots can "hide" within 300 imaginary cells large enough to hold the ship, as choices for locations before the bombs reach the surface.

In the dive on the cruiser, I was also thinking again about my boyhood participation in the manhunt for "Pretty Boy" Floyd. My father, as sheriff, deputized me along with a couple of dozen others to spread out and search the woods near Unionville where Floyd had been sighted. He, too, was banking on finding an air-cell in the forest where not one of the deputies could find him.

After I dropped my bomb, facing heavy anti-aircraft fire, I looked back to see the explosion—I had armed it for delayed action. Delayed action permitted the bomb to go far below decks where it would hit ammunitions storage and blow up the ship. I saw several explosions. The *Kinugasa* was sinking so rapidly that within minutes it was practically under water. Buchanan also scored a hit.

Meanwhile, as we retired from the enemy, I decided to head back to Henderson Field, knowing I didn't have enough gas to get back to the ship. At the same time as I was retiring from my strike, VB-10 Squadron Commander Tommy Thomas and the air group were coming in for their bombing runs on the same enemy fleet and saw the *Kinugasa* sinking. Another search pilot reported having seen the same cruiser sinking with two destroyers alongside picking up survivors.

The heavy cruiser *Kinugasa* was the flagship of Japanese Cruiser Division 6. She was providing cover for the troop reinforcement convoy by shelling Henderson Field. She previously served in the invasions of Guam and Wake Island, the landings in the Solomon Islands and New Guinea, and the battles of Coral Sea, Savo Island, and Cape Esperance. She capsized and sank at 11:22 a.m. southwest of Rendova Island, taking 511 crewman, including Captain Sawa, with her.

· 🍁 ·

JINK, JANK, JUNK

Jinking[57] out of an enemy fleet was the most exciting part of my day. It maybe even *made* my day. I read what was happening by watching the shells hit the water near me. If bullets were coming up at me from any direction, I knew it was time to turn one way. When I saw bullets coming down on me, I would turn the other way.

I also knew that when I saw anti-aircraft big black puffs fired at me at altitude, I headed for the puffs instantly while the bad guys changed their aim. I wanted to be where they were, not where they were going with their next shots. Flying toward flak requires being careful to reach it at just the right time—after the explosive energy is nearly spent, but the smoke hangs on. So I knew not to fly through explosions—only to fly through smoke.

When I got to Guadalcanal, the Japanese were shooting rifles at me as I came into the field. I made a right turn, and sort of a Split S, a flight maneuver that permits a sudden 180-degree reversal in direction, and then plunked down. So, we were under an air attack at the field, too. Before I came to a complete halt, my engine sputtered and died

---

57   This maneuver is the sudden, rapid displacement of the aircraft's flight path in three axes. This is used to confuse the enemy and prevent him from getting a good tracking solution, to avoid ground fire, or to avoid fragmentation patterns and ricochets. Navy Flight Manual, http://navyflightmanuals.tpub.com. To jerk an aircraft about in evasive action. *The US Air Force Dictionary*.

from lack of fuel. My plane revealed a number of holes, too, but the controls were in good shape, so I requested refueling and rearming.

A wild-eyed Marine about eighteen and suffering from malaria, dengue fever, and battle fatigue approached my plane. He looked like an old man. As I wrote earlier, all Marines were anxious to help us because we were keeping the enemy away from them. Marines had to refuel my plane with five-gallon gasoline cans and a crew quickly formed a bucket brigade to reload bombs and machine guns on my plane in addition to the needed gas.

Some other Marines came out in a Jeep and took me in to meet General Vandergrift, General Woods, and General Geiger. They took me to the underground Air Operations bunker near the pagoda the Japanese had built. I talked to them briefly and told them what I had seen, what was out there. Vandergrift asked if I wanted to go out with the Marines on a strike immediately. I said, "Absolutely. They are getting my plane ready and as soon as it is ready, I'll join the Marines in the air." This is what I came out here for. No Japanese will touch shore on Guadalcanal if I can help it!

The "Pagoda," used for base operations, was the most prominent structure on Henderson Field. (US Marine Corps, Thomas Carcelli Collection)

The total area the US controlled on Guadalcanal was a diameter of two miles around the center of the field, about 1,500 acres, the size of my hometown of Unionville, Missouri. As a real estate broker after the war, I learned how to appraise the value of land. Little did I know how vital and valuable those 1,500 acres were to the lives of so many fighting men and to the war in the Pacific. If we could hold them, they would become the most valuable acres in history.

When the Japanese bombing strike was completed, my plane was ready for action. The Marines were taking off and I followed them and joined up. With me, forming the last section of the flight, was Robbie from my squadron and another Marine. We climbed as we flew up *The Slot*. The Slot was the area between the islands of the Solomons that the Japanese came down each afternoon to shell Henderson Field after dark.

My three-plane section rendezvoused with the Marine aircraft [led by Maj. Robert H. Richard, VMSB-142] about two-thirds of the way up the Slot, arriving just in time. As we pulled into formation, Marine dive bombers started diving on the transports. The first fourteen bombers were all following the leader, Joe Sailer [Maj. Joseph Sailer, Jr, Commander, VMSB-132], who was quite a legend there at the time. He was a Marine dive bomber who had made a name for himself, just as Joe Foss, Marion Carl, and Pappy Boyington did flying fighters from the newly opened fighter strip.

There were several Marine hits on this one transport, and I thought, *Jesus Christ, they are all bombing one ship—it's been sunk four times already and they are still bombing it. Those stupid Marines!* The truth was and is that the military inhibits thinking so that few men adapt to a situation. However, those few who do adapt to a situation make the difference in outcomes. Few, if any, other countries than America have troops who can think on their feet.

Fortunately, I pulled my section of three planes over and picked the transport that was second from the front. I later learned it was the *Brisbane Maru*. As I came down in my dive, I could see that the deck was covered with men wearing khaki green and standing shoulder-to-shoulder.

Conditioned by three previous *baths-of-fire* while cowering from bombing and torpedo attacks by the enemy on two carriers, as well as receiving machine gun shells and cannon holes in my planes, I had no compunctions against shooting some more squirrels. Even as of this date, America was still losing the war and on the defensive, while hanging on desperately to a puny offensive position that could be lost on any one day. Our victory in the war was now my personal responsibility.

It was kill or be killed.

Following my bombing edict, I released a 1,000-pound bomb that hit the ship at midship in the epicenter of the troops, so as I pulled out I saw the ship break in two and sink immediately. Historians report this ship was the *Brisbane Maru*, and that this was the last ship sunk where the action was verified. The many sorties that followed during that day and the next left too vague a trail for accurate reporting.

Heading back to Guadalcanal uneventfully, I asked to get refueled and rearmed again. It was at this point that I first ran into the other members of my squadron, which included Tommy, my CO. He said, "What medal do you want? You can have your pick of any medal. We saw the cruiser sink."

I told him, "It doesn't matter. I'm not here for medals. Let's go out and sink some more ships while there're still some left."

Taking off from Henderson Field, Get in line! (US Marine Corps)
Note the perforated steel Marston Mat used for construction of
temporary runways and landing strips.

We went out late that afternoon. Tommy led the group. There were seven dive bombers from VB-10. Tommy climbed very slowly to the west with very little power. This was a trait that Tommy had shown since I joined his squadron. But when the leader of airplanes climbs and turns at slow speeds, he is seriously endangering the lives of the other pilots. The six planes behind can cut corners on the leader, but each successive plane is stuck to a slower speed to stay in formation. Barely flying above stalling speed reduces controls to a mushy feeling, the danger of falling out and hitting another plane, or of having another plane falling on you.

Hanging at low speeds, I was having trouble staying in formation behind him. We circled around and flew back and forth for almost half an hour while remaining way below an optimum starting diving altitude. I kept thinking, *Tommy, let's get our ass in there. The thing to do is, you get up to altitude, in as safe a position as possible. And in this case the enemy was only forty miles away. Then you come in at high speed, hit your target, and get your ass out of there. You don't fart around like this!*

I didn't know if Tommy was wounded, or what he was thinking in avoiding going in to hit the target, or what he was scared of, but it gave the Japanese exactly what they wanted—time to discover us—and we were hit by a whole swarm of Zeros who started shooting the crap out of us. Tommy and I would survive but many did not.

The Zeros shot five of our seven planes down. We were still short of the target at too low an altitude and at a miserable stalling speed. What a find for the Zeros. They made six or seven attack runs in rapid succession. We should have been in and out and home because the ships were only a few miles west of Guadalcanal. I reached a stalling speed and fell out of position in a spin. At the same time, I encountered a Japanese Zero coming at me head on from below. I fired my .50-caliber machine gun against his four machine guns and two canons in an unfair exchange. Bullets ripped through my controls and forced me out of position. I was in a bad spot. As he shot past me, I rolled from a spin into a dive.

We had been informed that the Zero would lose a wing if it rolled to the right at a speed of over 350 miles per hour. Knowing that the Zero would stick on to my tail, I decided to make a right aileron roll of 180 degrees and test the loss-of-wing theory. I was in a terminal velocity dive of over 400 miles per hour. I then realized that I was going to be pulling out heading toward Rabaul instead of Guadalcanal, but I said, "Oh, screw it!" and continued the roll to the right, making a full 360-degree roll.

Apparently, a Zero's wings don't pull off in right rolls at high speed because this one kept coming straight down and picked me up on the way out of the dive. The Zero pilot probably used his head and followed me without rolling until I had made my final commitment.

When I pulled out, he was still on my tail. I reached maximum speed during the dive and had all levers pushed toward the engine firewall—full throttle, high-blower, and high prop. Startled, I looked at the engine mercury-pressure gauge and it read 70 psi. *My God*, I thought, *the engine will explode!* Seventy pounds of pressure on the engine cylinders was well over the redline at 50 psi. After quickly pulling the levers back, the gauge dropped to 50 psi and I was safe again from that standpoint. But then there was the Zero.

I got into a horizontal position at a high rate of speed while feeling extreme G-forces. Even though the flight attitude of the plane was for level flight, the plane's true course was still downward. I thought, *Hell, I'm going to crash into the sea in spite of all of this!*

The plane mushed on, so that by the time I reached level flight, I was within twenty or thirty feet of the ocean. Split seconds counted again, and this became one of my miraculous escapes from death. The split seconds seemed like minutes. My awareness was at an unbelievable height. By luck, I had managed to pull out of the dive and stay alive. The Japanese Zero was still on my tail and firing. I could see and feel bullets and canon shells hitting my wings, fuselage, and underneath my seat. I began jinking.

I knew enough about gunnery to know to get on a target you have to come in on it at a rate of speed that gives you a chance to fire at the target in accordance with its flight path. I figured this man was hot on my tail, but he couldn't come in from below me because I was never more than fifty feet from the water, zig-zagging back and forth, and up and down. He didn't have a chance to come in from afar and estimate my fight path.

I couldn't let the Zero stay sitting on my tail for any length of time, giving the pilot a chance to determine my flight pattern in order to fire to kill me. He couldn't read my flight path because I was flying in an ever-changing left/right skid. My needle-ball indicator was flying radically from one extreme to the other. Since I couldn't out-run him, the slower I went the more difficult his task became. Slipping through exaggerated left-right skids burned speed at a fast rate.

That being the case, he couldn't come in from behind and keep hitting, he couldn't come in from a distance because I was hugging the ocean, and he had no room to recover from a dive. Most frustrating of all, he couldn't measure my path because it was constantly changing. He had to sit on my tail at a dangerously slow speed for him, reduced to very short firing periods that enhanced my chances to skid through his fire with less hazard. As I saw his bullets tear into my wing and work toward the cockpit, I would slam full rudder and full opposite stick, lift my exposed leg, and let the bullets come through and die at the firewall.

I thought, *Every time you're close to death, time stands still.* When you're in danger of death, the seconds lengthen into minutes. Movement of action becomes very vivid, moves slowly, and is more understandable. Yes, all of a sudden, things become very clear as they move very slowly. I was confident I was doing the right thing—and that I would live. He would quickly run out of ammo.

And he did run out of ammo, and I did live. Caught in situations like this, you cannot rely on stuff you read in books. Inspiration flashes up like a bright light. I didn't know exactly when I was going to get out of the hole, but I knew what was happening, and that the time frame for my actions was working to my benefit.

I kept jinking and it finally did the trick. With our plane riddled and vapor trails of fuel spraying from all four of our tanks, I thought the Jap pilot must be thoroughly dismayed that I was still flying. The Zero then flew up on us as if flying in formation, just a few feet off my left wingtip. The two of us flew straight ahead while we looked eyeball to eyeball for more than a minute. I had everything firewalled for maximum speed but when he decided to leave, he rocked his wings. I waved and off he went. Jamming on his throttle, he rapidly and smoothly pulled up into an Immelman—a half loop followed by a slow roll—now a thousand feet above me and headed home.

•　❧　•

The Zeros were from the *Hiyo* under the command of veteran Lt. Cdr. Kaneko Tadashi. Tadishi himself led his wingman Chief Petty Officer Tanaka Jiro in the attack. Tanaka went after Hoot and got twenty-seven shells into his Dauntless before Schindele hit Tanaka's Zero. "Tanaka flew alongside Gibson for a few minutes, barely a yard off of his wing. After looking each other eyeball to eyeball for more than a minute, Tanaka waved his wings in a sign of respect for Gibson's flying ability, which Gibson returned with a wave. Then Tanaka flew off, eventually ditching. Gibson nursed his Dauntless back to Henderson, where mechanics "just looked at it and shoved it over into the graveyard ditch. It wasn't worth repairing.'"[58]

•　❧　•

Landing back on Guadalcanal, I took a close look at my gunner Schindele, who was unscathed except for a bullet scratch on one leg. We both laughed together at each other while the ground crew counted sixty-eight holes in the plane. Each of the four gas tanks had been hit by 20 mm canon shells where gas had been pouring out in streams during flight. I had noticed that as the gas escaped, it vaporized and left four jet streams trailing the plane. Many of the machine-gun bullets had entered my cockpit on an angle that would have hit my legs had

---

58　Cox, *Blazing Star, Setting Sun,* 188-189.

I not lifted the proper leg at the proper time. That reaction, however, had not taken a rocket scientist. The Marines pushed the plane into the graveyard ditch and took us to our quarters. I have often wondered what was going through Schindele's head in the rear cockpit during that Zero encounter. Neither one of us ever asked.

•　❖　•

"The Zero used up all its ammunition without destroying Gibson's plane and then did the only decent thing I ever heard of a Jap soldier doing. He flew alongside Gibson's plane and dipped his wings in admission of defeat."

—Chicago Sun-Times, June 21, 1943

•　❖　•

Cactus Air Force SBD and TBF planes lined up at Henderson Field on November 14, 1942 (US Marine Corps)

The next day I led a flight to bomb one of the beached transports. As we crossed from the tent area to the operations area near the old pagoda, the Japanese on the hill across the river a mile away were lobbing shells in from five-inch mortars. After running about twenty to thirty feet, I could hear a shell coming at me and would hit the deck. The old saying was that *You never hear the one that hits you*, but why take any chance? I remember the ground was sort of muddy and dusty at the same time. It was the one place reported you could stand in the mud up to your rear end and have dust blowing in your face.

On that flight I bombed a transport [*Kunigawa Maru*] being unloaded on the beach. Again, this time I apparently hit other ammunition because there were two huge explosions—one vertical and one came horizontally out of the port midship side of the transport.

The *Kinugawa Maru*, beached on Guadalcanal at the mouth of the Bonegi River near Tassafaronga. (National Archives). The carcass of the ship remains there today.

Returning to the field just a few miles away, Schindele took the famous picture below showing four transports burning with my wing plane blocking the sun in a dramatic manner. The picture was printed in *Life* magazine as one of the top ten war pictures of 1942.

Photo Taken from Bob Gibson's SBD, this view shows several Japanese troop ships burning on the beach off the coast of Guadalcanal on the afternoon of November 15, 1942. (US Navy)

· ✳ ·

THE EVER-PRESENT GIBSON

Hoot's exploits on November 14-15, 1942 off of Santa Cruz are legendary and are described by eminent chroniclers as beyond heroic—epic. It is wise to start with the official US Navy historian Samuel Eliot Morison, who aptly described Guadalcanal as a campaign that "never inspired much laughter."Morison reports that Hoot's and Buchanan's scout planes were launched at 8:06 a.m. as part of the search group from *Enterprise* on the morning of November 14 to cover a northwesterly sector for 200 miles out and eight planes to cover a northerly sector for 250 miles out. "Ten fighters and seventeen dive-bombers armed with 1,000-pound bombs were ready on the flight deck. At 7:08 a.m. one of the search planes reported ten unidentified planes 140 miles to the northward, flying towards *Enterprise*. What these planes were never was ascertained, but the report caused Captain Hardison to head into the wind and launch his attack group with instructions to head north, look, and listen." This early departure ended up being good luck when Ensign Bob Gibson's contact report came through: "Two battleships, two heavy cruisers, one possible converted carrier, four destroyers, position 8 45′ S, 157° 10′E, course 290°.[59] While Hoot and Buchanan "took a crack at *Kinugasa*, which started flooding and gave the heavy cruiser a ten-degree list, Lieutenant Commander James R. Lee in command of the *Enterprise* attack group was making a beeline for the enemy."[60]

Noted *Enterprise* historian Eugene Burns—author of the engaging 1944 book *Then There Was One*—dramatically set the stage for Hoot's adventure. "Aboard the *Enterprise* the next morning, Friday, November 14, two hours before daybreak Lieutenant (j.g.) Robert D. Gibson was wakened. Gibson was a tall, soft-spoken, blue-eyed flier from Unionville, Missouri. He had had an excellent musical training and could play anything from a French horn to a piccolo. His flying and fighting, like his ability to play the piano, were first rate. Bob took off at daybreak with Clifford E. Schindele, his rearseatman." [61]

Burns describes the action as Bob flew to the end of his search sector without result. "[Bob] was not satisfied with that and radioed his wingman, Ensign Buchanan. 'I know damn well that there are Japs around here. I can smell them. Let's stretch here some more,' he said. 'Roger,' said Buchanan, accepting. Gibson and Buchanan were rewarded. The two pilots looked to the south of the New Georgia island group and there, 150 miles west of Guadalcanal, big as life, was a cruiser force of eleven ships—three light cruisers, three heavy cruisers, and five destroyers."

Bob made eight separate reports on the disposition and composition of the Japanese force, "while the Japs in turn threw up everything they

---

59   Radio report of Lt. (j.g.) Robert D. Gibson USNR of VB-10 at 0915; Enterprise Action Report.

60   Morison, *The Struggle for Guadalcanal*, 264-265.

61   Eugene Burns, *Then There Was One: The U.S.S. Enterprise and the First Year of the War*, New York: Harcourt, Brace, 1944, 150-153. The quoted passages in the following paragraphs from Burns are not separately noted but are contained within this note's referenced text.

had to drive him away." As their gas supply was running low, it was time to act. Gibson and Buchanan climbed to 17,000 feet where they selected their targets, a heavy cruiser of the *Nachi* class. Burns writes that Gibson called to Buchanan: "Here goes," and put his plane into a steep dive, with Buchanan following by seconds. The explosion, according to rearseatman Schindele, "picked up the whole ship and set it over about six feet." Then, as Gibson pulled out, Schindele strafed until they got out of range. Buchanan also got a direct hit, and flew away, the heavy cruiser burning behind them.

Bob then radioed the Big E with the news of the first attack of the day. "When it was relayed over the loudspeaker system, *Enterprise* men cheered."

Bob and Buchanan headed to Henderson Field and came in on fumes while the field was under Japanese attack. Bob immediately asked that his plane be refueled and armed and took off from Henderson Field within twenty-five minutes with a squadron of Marine pilots. They were off to attack a transport group that had been reported by Lieutenant Carmody of the *Enterprise*.

Burns continues the narrative. "Zeros notwithstanding, Gibson got a hit on a median-sized transport of about 8,000 tons. 'I did not notice the troops on it,' he said, 'until we got in close because the ship's color and their clothes blended. They were close packed.' During their departure, Schindele shot down a Zero and then once again took pictures which showed the transport burning fiercely."

Gibson and Schindele returned to Guadalcanal where they once again armed, gassed, and returned to the fight. However, this time they rejoined seven other *Enterprise* pilots. "As they prepared for the attack, a large force of Jap Zeros intercepted them. Gibson's airplane was badly damaged and it went out of control temporarily, the plane falling like a dead duck. "I was hit and had to fall out," said Gibson. "As I was falling, I managed to release my bomb. Then I got my controls back. But just as I pulled out, a Zero got on my wing. He rode on it for ten miles, giving me bursts. My rear guns were jammed so the Zero didn't have any opposition. . . . He only knocked out my control cable and put a few holes in my plane."

Burns reports that "Gibson's squadron commander, Lieutenant Commander John A. Thomas, corrected that one. 'A few holes! God Almighty! Every one of your tanks was punctured and the sides of your fuselage were riddled!'"

Stanley Johnston, the noted historian who wrote *The Grim Reapers* in 1943 while embedded with the famous *Enterprise* fighter squadrons writes that "The *Enterprise* scouts, not quite a hundred miles ahead of this formation, meanwhile made contact with and engaged the Japanese transports. Lieutenant Robert ("Hoot") Gibson of Unionville, Missouri, and R. M. Buchanan sighted the enemy past New Georgia Island. Clifford Schindele, Gibson's rear gunner, radioed the force's position, course, speed, number, and types. Hoot and Buchanan then continued their search for bigger game." [62]

Johnston interviewed Bob. Here is Bob's account from the interview:

We were seeking the main enemy fleet, which was believed to be lurking somewhere in this area. After passing around the southwestern end of New Georgia, we sighted a force of six cruisers and five destroyers. The cruisers steamed in two columns of three ships each. There were a lot of broken clouds. After making the initial contact report, we continued the search in the hope of locating a flat-top.

We searched for forty-five minutes. The hostile ships fired at us whenever we passed within range and we made use of the broken clouds to make it awkward for the gunners to get a good shot at our planes. Since we'd been ordered to await an acknowledgment of our contact report before attacking or leaving any enemy force, we idled around. Later, I discovered that my receiver had gone haywire and I couldn't pick up the signal.

After about an hour of this, our gasoline was getting dangerously low, so Buchanan and I decided to climb for diving altitude and attack the cruiser force below. When we

62   Stanley Johnston, *The Grim Reapers*, New York: E.P. Dutton, 1943, 174-178.

got into position, we waited for a favorable cloud break. Then we let down, with our noses pointed right at the biggest cruiser, a heavy *Nachi* class. From training and experience, I knew how difficult it is for gunners to hit a dive bomber coming down almost directly from above, and though I didn't like the heavy anti-aircraft guns, I didn't much worry about them while we were diving from the 12,000 to the 6,000-foot section. But once we passed below that level and into the range of the light automatics, it got dangerous enough.

The size of the victim grew in the sights until I could see its deck clearly. When my altimeter registered 1,000 feet, I squeezed the bomb release lever and the 1,000-pounder fell away. Then I pulled out of the dive and began to retire.

Buchanan was right astern and let his bomb go a couple seconds later. Schindele, who was shooting its machine guns into the cruiser as I pulled away, saw our bomb hit and erupt violently on the starboard side, right amidships. The shock of the explosion seemed to jerk the cruiser violently, Buchanan's bomb exploded slightly abaft amidships, on the port side.

My gunner switched from his machine guns to his camera and took about two hundred feet of film of the mounting fire aboard the cruiser as we withdrew.[63]

Johnston then questioned Hoot about the length of time he figured he was being shot at while making the attack. Bob replied:

The actual dive takes no more than twenty seconds, but they are a long twenty seconds for the pilot and radioman. Getting away takes longer still. Usually, we don't steer directly away from the ship because that would give the gunners an easy shot at us. In this particular case we didn't' have to worry about the victim's fire because every gun stopped shooting

---

63   Ibid.

immediately when our bombs exploded. But this did not prevent the other ships from shooting at us. I steered a course roughly slanting, and occasionally zigzagging, to make the shot more difficult. Within perhaps fifteen seconds, we were out of the Jap's small-arms fire, but their heavies continued to shoot for perhaps a half a minute." [64]

Beached Japanese troop transport ships *Hirokawa Maru* and *Kinugawa Maru* burn from bomb damage off Guadalcanal. Photo taken from Bob Gibson's SBD on November 15, 1942.

Historian and fellow naval aviator Commander Edward P. Stafford details Bob Gibson's exploits from Henderson Field in his fine history of the *Enterprise* entitled *The Big E*. "At 12:20 p.m., Gibson and Buchanan were circling waiting to land after their five-hour morning search and their attack on the cruiser force. Thirty-five minutes later Hoot Gibson was back in the air headed for the transports as part of the seventeen-Dauntless attack group. On his wing flew Ensign Len Robinson, and Marine Sergeant Beneke was the third SBD in the section. As they approached the advancing troopships, a Zero curved in behind and under Robinson firing steadily and pulling up. The blade antenna mast mounted just in

---

64   Id.

front of Robinson's face between cockpit and engine was chopped off and flew up and back over his head. Gibson could see holes in the bottom of Robinson's wings. Schindele in Gibson's rear seat drove the Zero off with his twin 30s just before the section pushed over."[65]

Stafford continues: "From 6,000 feet down the AA was heavy and accurate, the tracers whipping past close aboard and the heavy bursts jarring the crosshairs off the target. Gibson and Robinson in reply strafed with their two fixed guns, and Gibson did well in the afternoon with his 1,000-pounder as he had in the morning with his 500. He planted it dead amidships. Robinson five seconds later put his in nearly the same hole. Sergeant Beneke, as he dropped his close in, watched the big transport crack in half, her back broken, men and equipment spilling from the edges of the break. All three planes strafed the wreck as they pulled away close to the surface of the sea."

Stafford then reports on Hoot's third flight of the day. This one at 4:30 p.m. with his fellow *Enterprise* attack group under Lieutenant Commander Thomas's Bombing Ten. "Thomas took his squadron in bare. He had Dauntlesses in two sections. It no longer required much flying to find the transports and before 5:00 p.m., the VB-10 pilots at 12,000 feet had them in sight. The five big ships were still underway and pushing for Guadalcanal. Astern of them others lay dead in the water or burning and one or two seemed to be headed west. As Thomas picked up his mike to assign targets, the seven Dauntlesses were suddenly smothered by Zeros."

Stafford's describes the ensuing fight. "A dozen of the clean, low-winged fighters dived in on the port side of the bomber formation. . . . Hoot Gibson on the extreme left was the first target of the Japanese and Schindele in his rear seat swung his twin 30s out to port to meet them. Two of the enemy concentrated on Gibson; Schindele hit one and he slanted off, smoke trailing from his engine, but Gibson's Dauntless was badly holed and spun out of formation. With full forward stick and stiff-

---

65   Commander Edward P. Stafford, *The Big E: The Story of the USS Enterprise*, Naval Institute Press: Annapolis, 1962, 220-242. The quoted passages in the following paragraphs from Stafford are not separately noted but are contained within this note's referenced text.

legged full opposite rudder, he fought the spin until the rugged little SBD came out in a swooping glide close to the water. Riddled, with leaking tanks and most of his systems out, Gibson decided he had used up his quota of luck for the fourteenth of November and concentrated on getting back to Henderson in one piece. With the free guns jammed and a Zero on his tail he hedgehopped across the Russell Islands, dodging and weaving like a tired boxer until the Zero ran out of ammunition and turned away."

Stafford also reports that two days later on November 16, at 11:30, "Thomas, Gibson, Goddard, and Robinson took off on a search for [Tiny] Carroum and any other survivors of the action in the Slot. They swept in low and slow over the Russells [Islands], scanning the beaches, bays, and inlets, and looking for a white face among the black upturned ones in native villages. Hoot Gibson found one white man and dropped him dungarees and cigarettes, but he was not from Bombing Six or *Enterprise*."

Finally, historian Barrett Tillman describes Hoot's action on the morning of November 14: "Diving from astern, the Dauntless pair put both 500-pounders close aboard, opening seams to port and destroying the ship's steering. It was fatal damage. Incredibly, Buchanan's plane took a main-battery round through the tail, leaving an eight-inch hole where the shell failed to detonate. During the egress, Gibson laid the stick over and kicked the rudder pedals, offering the most difficult target possible. He said, 'When you're jinking out of an enemy fleet, it's the most exciting part of your day.' The ever-present Gibson headed for Henderson."[66]

· ❉ ·

LITMUS TEST

One of those days at Guadalcanal, while waiting for my dive bomber to be gassed and armed for the next flight, I hitched a short Jeep ride to the east end of the airstrip to view the Japanese prisoner stockade. There I saw a strange sight as a Marine guard threw his bayonet over

---

66   Tillman, 141.

the stockade fence, whereupon a prisoner picked it up and threw it back to the Marine. It was a 1942 litmus test. I was told that if the prisoners tried to conceal the weapon they would be shot.

I was amused. The litmus test asked, "How are you prisoners going to behave?" It was a test much like politicians today want to use to control Supreme Court nominees.

Real estate on Guadalcanal was tightly held, and square footages changed constantly. It was not unusual for a takeoff to be delayed while dead Japanese were dragged from the runway. It somehow reminded me of my father's takeoffs and landings over cows, instead of dead bodies, on the runway back home in Unionville.

· ❧ ·

RECOVERY AND AFTERMATH

We operated for several days out of Guadalcanal bombing shipping and land bases. We also made many flights in vain looking for pilots who had been shot down. It is extremely difficult to sight objects or people on the vast ocean.

We had PBYs and OS2U sea planes, with floats, that were picking up pilots, just as in the aftermath of Midway. It was probably not until the beginning of 1943 that we had the strength and ability to develop any kind of rescue. For the most part the rule for the total year of 1942 was if a pilot was lost or shot down in a life raft, his chances were less than 50 percent of getting picked up. If he managed to land someplace, sometime later he might get returned back to the allies. Of those in life rafts at sea who didn't make it to land in 1942, not more than 25 percent were picked up.

The pickup factor increased dramatically in 1943 and through 1945. Air and sea rescue devised radio transmitters for pilots in downed planes. In 1942, our rescue kit was comprised primarily of a mirror to signal an airplane. We also carried an edible bar, which was a dry sort of fruit for food, and two or three canteens of water good for five days at most.

At a later date when I got lost, I figured there was no way I could reach an island. One of our pilots swam for seventy-two hours, though, and finally reached one. He was picked up several days later by a seaplane. The pilot brought with him a letter written by the native chief, addressed to President Roosevelt, inviting him to come visit the chief.

Shortly thereafter the group of pilots in Bombing Ten were loaded on board a DC3 and flown south to the New Hebrides Islands. We arrived there a couple of days before the *Enterprise* and its fleet came into harbor. We were based on an island named Esprito Santos in the northern part of the islands several hundred miles south of Guadalcanal.

By that time the Navy was feeling confident enough that they had moved the base of operations for advanced areas from New Caledonia up to the New Hebrides Islands where Esprito had the best natural harbor. South Pacific command, however, remained in New Caledonia.

Tommy Thomas, who had survived the zero attack, and I each flew a plane down to Tontuta in New Caledonia with a stop at Efate on the way for gas and for an interview with Admiral Halsey.

Admiral "Bull" Halsey ordered me to fly to New Caledonia to brief him at his headquarters about the battle at Guadalcanal. He said to me: "You can have any medal you want" and mentioned the Medal of Honor. I said, "No, that would not be fair to the six pilots in my squadron that were killed. That medal is for foot soldiers that throw their bodies on hand grenades. Besides, I don't want any medal. I am a highly paid ($250 per month), highly trained professional, and I am satisfied with staying alive. Thank you." Halsey later gave me the Navy Cross, but I did not ask for it.

· 🍀 ·

For his service Hoot received the Navy Cross for his actions during the Third Defense of Guadalcanal on November 14-15, 1942.

THE SECRETARY OF THE NAVY
WASHINGTON

The President of the United States takes pleasure in presenting the NAVY CROSS to

LIEUTENANT JUNIOR GRADE ROBERT D. GIBSON
UNITED STATES NAVAL RESERVE

for service as set forth in the following

CITATION:

"For extraordinary heroism in the line of his profession as a Bombing Pilot of the U.S.S. ENTERPRISE during the engagement with enemy Japanese naval and air forces in the Solomon Islands Area on November 14 and 15, 1942. With utter disregard for his own personal safety, Lieutenant (junior grade) Gibson made, and skillfully developed, contact with a large force of enemy cruisers and destroyers. Attacking a Nachi-class heavy cruiser and several enemy transports, he scored a direct hit on the cruiser and on a transport. After his plane had destroyed one Zero-type fighter and hit another, he brought his ship gallantly through the engagement, although badly damaged by enemy fire. The next day, returning to attack a beached Japanese transport, he bombed and exploded it. His remarkable courage, expert skill and fearless devotion to duty were an inspiration to his men and in keeping with the highest traditions of the United States Naval Service."

For the President,

Frank Knox
Secretary of the Navy.

Hoot receiving Navy Cross from Rear Adm. John Downes

* ❧ *

In the three-day struggle known to history as the Naval Battle of Guadalcanal, the Japanese navy had been soundly defeated and driven back up the Slot.[67] The Americans would stick at Hell's Island . . . and go on the offensive.

* ❧ *

---

67   Toll, *The Conquering Tide*, 174.

UNITED STATES NAVAL CHRONOLOGY WORLD WAR II

NOVEMBER 1942

12 THU. Naval Battle of Guadalcanal (12-15 November) opens as transports (Rear Adm. R. K. Turner) unloading troops in Lunga Roads, Guadalcanal, Solomon Islands, under the protection of air and surface forces, are attacked by Japanese aircraft.

UNITED STATES NAVAL VESSELS DAMAGED:
- Heavy cruiser *San Francisco* (CA-38) by aircraft
- Destroyer *Buchanan* (DD-484) accidently by US naval gunfire

13 FRI. Landing Support Group (Rear Adm. D. J. Callaghan) encounters Japanese Raiding Group, including two battleships, steaming to bombard Henderson Field, Guadalcanal, a devastating naval action ensues in the darkness off Guadalcanal, Solomon Islands. Heavy damage is inflicted on United States forces in naval action in the darkness off Guadalcanal, Solomon Islands. Japanese Raiding Group retires northward. Carrier force (Rear Adm. T. C. Kinkaid) arrives close to battle area and launches air search and attacks against the enemy.

UNITED STATES NAVAL VESSELS SUNK:
- Light cruiser *Atlanta* (CL-51) by naval gunfire
- Light cruiser *Juneau* (CL-52) by submarine torpedo
- Destroyer *Cushing* (DD-376) by naval gunfire
- Destroyer *Monssen* (DD-436) by naval gunfire
- Destroyer *Laffey* (DD-459) by gunfire and torpedo for surface craft.
- Destroyer *Barton* (DD-599) by torpedo from surface craft

UNITED STATES NAVAL VESSELS DAMAGED:
- Heavy cruiser *Portland* (CA-33) by torpedo from surface craft
- Heavy cruiser *San Francisco* (CA-38) by naval gunfire

UNITED STATES NAVAL VESSELS DAMAGED (CONT.):
- Light cruiser *Helena* (CL-50) by naval gunfire
- Destroyer *Sterett* (DD-407) by naval gunfire
- Destroyer *O'Bannon* (DD-450) accidentally by US naval gunfire
- Destroyer *Aaron Ward* (DD-483) by naval gunfire

JAPANESE NAVAL VESSELS SUNK:
- Battleship *Hiei*, by naval gunfire, carrier-based and Marine land-based aircraft
- Destroyer *Akatsuki*, by naval gunfire
- Destroyer *Yudachi*, by naval gunfire

14 SAT. Japanese cruisers and destroyers engaged in night bombardment of Henderson Field, Guadalcanal, Solomon Islands, are attacked by motor torpedo boats. In the morning this enemy force, while retiring, is struck by Marine aircraft from Henderson Field, and naval aircraft from carrier *Enterprise* (CV-6). Seven Japanese transports are sunk.

UNITED STATES NAVAL VESSELS SUNK:
- Destroyer *Preston* (DD-379) by naval gunfire
- Destroyer *Walke* (DD-416) by gunfire and torpedo from surface vessel

JAPANESE NAVAL VESSEL SUNK:
- Heavy cruiser *Kinugasa* by naval aircraft

15 SUN. Naval Battle of Guadalcanal ends.

UNITED STATES NAVAL VESSEL SUNK:
- Destroyer *Benham* (DD-397) damaged by torpedo and sunk by US forces

UNITED STATES NAVAL VESSELS DAMAGED:
- Battleship *South Dakota* (BB-57), by naval gunfire
- Destroyer *Gwin* (DD-433) by naval gunfire

JAPANESE NAVAL VESSELS SUNK:
- Battleship *Kirishima* by naval gunfire
- Destroyer Ayanami, by naval gunfire

CHAPTER EIGHT

NEW HEBRIDES AND RETURN TO PEARL HARBOR

Save the Chicago*!*

A Douglas SBD flies over USS *Enterprise* (CV-6) and USS *Saratoga* (CV-3) on December 19, 1942 (US Navy National Naval Aviation Museum)

NEW HEBRIDES

Following our arrival in New Hebrides Island in late 1942, Bill Martin took a TBF to Nouméa where he picked up a fifty-five-gallon drum of rum. This was used as the basis for establishing the bar and beach club. The fleet established another officers club at the fleet landing, a twenty-minute drive away from our bomber strip. The fleet landing O'Club was sort of unusual. The manager would get a shipment each day from certain ships that included a limited number of bottles of rum, and some bottles of bourbon, gin, scotch, and a few cases of beer. When the bar opened at one o'clock, only gin was served, at two only beer, at three it was rum and at four it was bourbon.

The drinking schedule was changed every day. By the time five o'clock came around it was time to go back to the dock and everyone was drunk. There, at the dock, while waiting for a barge from various ships, many engaged in fist fights and would occasionally fall into the ocean. When it is impossible to fight the enemy, we fight each other.

Pretending to be a little higher in class, Air Group 10 decided we'd have our own bar. Proximity was paramount. A tent was assigned to such proper duty, and the B&B, (bar and beach club) came into being on the beach after we snitched an ice maker from aboard the ship. Surrounding the club were coconut groves and a grove of lime trees. That gave all the ingredients—a fifty-five-gallon drum of rum, limes, water, and ice. So, a customer would step up and order "I'll have one of the usual," meaning that he'd have one of the only kind of drink available.

The coconut plantation surrounding the living quarters was infested with rats, so one of the games we played when we came back from the officer's club half-drunk was to sneak into the hut with our .45 revolvers ready while one man turned on the lights and we'd pot-shoot rats. One night I felt this body crawling over mine, so I took the sheet, flung it out, and heard a rat hit the wall. I guess it made him mad because he came back, jumped up on me, and tried to bite me. I really let him have it. Even old Ed Christie, owner of the Staples

Hotel back home in Unionville, would have agreed that this rat fight was more like a bull fight!

We played a similar game later on while stationed at Corpus Christi, Texas, where the cockroaches were bad. We slipped into the house at night and made a weapon of a rolled-up newspaper. Then we flicked on the lights to see who could kill the most cockroaches before they all disappeared.

Back to New Hebrides, now the country called Vanuatu.

The bomber strip there was also used by the Air Corps. They had B17s that were dropping bombs someplace each day. When the 17s came in, any bombs they had not used that day were tossed out to one side of the plane. One night when a crowd was at the movies—the seats at the movies were coconut trees where everyone would sit on a log— some jerk came in late and saw that there weren't any log seats left, so he got a 100-pound bomb from one of the B17s and was dragging it over by its tail to sit on. The bomb exploded and killed about thirty guys. One of my good friends, Bud Lucier, was pelted with shrapnel and was in the hospital for a considerable period of time. For the next twenty-five years, he had pieces of shrapnel working their way out of his body. Operating techniques were not the best then, and it was considered safer to leave shrapnel in a body than to cut it out.

These were some of the exciting activities during the interim between periods of combat. Believe me, as raucous as this lifestyle sounds, it was tame compared to the sheer terror we felt while engaged in battle.

For instance, right in front of our hut was a beautiful ocean lagoon with crystal-clear water where you could see to the ocean bottom. The bottom, however, was covered with a dangerously sharp coral surface. If you went out in the water, you wore tennis shoes or your feet would be sliced to ribbons. Wearing tennis shoes, we had a ton of fun diving between the coral reefs and finding caves where millions of multi-colored fish held sway. We devised some fish-spears for waging many unsuccessful, but vigorous attempts at landing a prize.

Not far away was an anti-aircraft battery company. We mentioned our failure in fish-spearing to some of the battery officers who said, "We've got a better way if you want some fish." The two factions rendezvoused and one of the men took a few sticks of dynamite out into the ocean and stuck it down into one of these holes that we'd been fishing in. A line was strung back to the shore and one army officer exploded the charge. Whereupon the surface of the ocean was covered with stunned fish.

We all dashed out with gunnysacks, scooped up the harvest and promptly took it to the Army installation. The reward was an invitation to a fish fry! That was in 1942. Strangely, in June of 1978, I was in Kansas City at a party with a group of attorneys and one man said, "Hell, I remember you! I was the officer who blew up the fish." I hadn't seen him in all those years.

Many other activities were going on in the New Hebrides, too. The Marines had a fighter strip a few miles north of us where they had found a huge, deep lagoon filled with clear water. It was in an idealistic setting that permitted us to climb up a high bank, with huge vines three to four inches in diameter hanging from the trees. You could jump off the bank, swing on the vine out over the pool, and drop in. We often tried after a Tarzan-like swim there to invade the Marines' officers club and drink up all their booze.

At one point half a dozen Army nurses showed up on the scene and, of course, several thousand crazy men, who hadn't seen a woman for many months, were there waiting and foaming at the mouth. Competition was pretty tough to get a chance with any of these girls. We managed to get such a chance by gathering a collection of hairpins—fashioned and made aboard ship, where we also stole some pillows—and went over in the jeep to make our presentations. Thus, we managed to get in ahead of most of the guys to at least talk to the girls.

Another interesting part of life in New Hebrides was very slight contact with the natives or with the French and English traders. The natives had a practice of catching wild pigs to tether to a stake in their village. Each day the natives would massage the tusk of a wild boar from the time it was a small piglet to make the tusk curve. By the time the pig was full sized, they had a tusk that made a perfect bracelet to sell to the crazy Americans.

Our flight training continued as well. Again, we received replacement pilots and new aircraft. About 150 miles south of us was a huge, active volcano, so one day our squadron flew down to take a look close up. I was leading the flight that day as we came in from the western side, swept down into the bowl of the volcano Aoba and flew the entire diameter hundreds of feet below the edge of the volcano. Its surface had huge deposits of yellow sulfur and other red minerals, along with smoke oozing up. It was smoldering at that time, but I had seen it from a distance, when it was actively erupting.

During the rest of the flight, I led the squadron down to a French planter's town, Port Vila, on the island of Efate. Port Vila was the capital of the New Hebrides. We landed there at noon and found maybe twenty French people who were living there with about 400 natives. It was a little trading post, with a couple of bars. That enticed us to sit around and get half gassed on beer, until it was time to fly back on a night flight, as we had planned. Fortunately, the squadron returned without incident, but did enjoy the flight immensely under a full tropical moon.

Hoot (front row fourth from left); Bombing Ten, New Hebrides (US Navy)

There were constant sorties where the *Enterprise* steamed back up to the Solomon Islands, keeping to the east or south, and we'd hit land targets and search the area. This went on for a period of months. By late January the Japanese had decided that they would pull out of Guadalcanal, so by early February 1943, the last of the 11,000 starving troops were evacuated. Without more opposition, Guadalcanal was secured, and the outcome of the Pacific war was decided. Both the Japanese and the Americans knew it, too.

· ❀ ·

BATTLE OF RENNELL ISLAND

On January 14, 1943, a Japanese convoy stealthily delivered a battalion of troops to act as a rear guard for the evacuation of Japanese forces from Guadalcanal. At the same time, Japanese warships and aircraft moved into position around the Rabaul and Bougainville areas in preparation to execute the withdrawal operation. Allied intelligence detected the Japanese movements but misinterpreted them as preparations for another attempt to retake Henderson Field and Guadalcanal.

On January 29, Halsey, acting on the same intelligence, sent a resupply convoy to Guadalcanal screened by a cruiser task force. Sighting the cruisers, Japanese naval torpedo bombers attacked that same evening and heavily damaged the cruiser *Chicago*. The next day, despite determined efforts by escort warships and pilots from the *Enterprise* to save the wounded *Chicago*, more torpedo aircraft attacked and sank *Chicago*. Halsey ordered the remainder of the task force to return to base and directed the rest of his naval forces to take station in the Coral Sea, south of Guadalcanal, to be ready to counter a Japanese offensive.

· ❀ ·

SAVE THE *CHICAGO*

In late January 1943, I was sent on a search to find the USS *Chicago*, a heavy cruiser in Task Force 18. It had been badly damaged in surface action as part of the Battle of Rennell Island. After locating *Chicago* in my search sector, I directed a team of F4Fs to fly air patrol to protect the cruiser. There was concern that a bombing attack might come in to finish off the ship.

Other authors have detailed the mission:

· 🍀 ·

"CHICAGO DAMAGED AND UNDER TOW OF LOUISVILLE IN POSITION . . ."

Operations Order 2-43, January 30, 1943; Rear Adm. Frederick Sherman, Carrier Division 2, Fast Carrier Task Force.

· 🍀 ·

Commander Edward Stafford describes the search for the USS *Chicago*:

When Sherman's Operation Order 2-43 went into effect, *Enterprise* was some 350 miles south and slightly west of the crippled heavy cruiser *Chicago*. Task Force 16 turned north at sixteen knots.

In the predawn dark just before 6:00 a.m., the first planes left the Big E's deck. Hoot Gibson and Red Hoogerwerf, Buell and Frissel, in two search sections of SBDs, fanned out to locate *Chicago*. Gibson located the damaged heavy cruiser at 7:15, some thirty-five miles north of the eastern tip of Rennell. She was down by the stern and trailing a broad, iridescent river of oil. *Louisville*, at the other end of a long catenary of anchor chain and towing cable, was easing her southeastward toward Espiritu at about four knots. *Wichita* steamed slowly to starboard of the other two heavy cruisers, and the three light cruisers patrolled back and forth to port. The eight destroyers chased tails around the heavy ships and a fleet tug with her high bow and low stern was approaching *Louisville* to take over the tow.

Hoot at once transmitted the force position to Flatley's fighters, then dropped dive rakes and flew slowly over *Louisville* giving his gunner a "mark" to throw down a beanbag with a message giving the Wildcat radio frequency. At eight o'clock as Hoot and Hooger left to find the escort carriers, six of the VF-10s blunt-winged Wildcats swung into position overhead.

Gibson found the two stubby little [escort] carriers [*Chenanga* and *Suwannee*] with their thin island structure and high sides thirty minutes away. The four men in the two Dauntlesses looked these strange craft over with interest, noting the short, wide decks, their unsteady motion, and were glad they were flying from the *Enterprise* with her thirty knots and her long deck bordered with gun barrels. Gibson dropped another message requesting the frequency of the small carrier's fighters and then circled slowly while the answer came back by flashing light from high in the island.[68]

· ❦ ·

Navy historian Steve Ewing provides more details once Hoot located the *Chicago*:

At 7:15 a.m., Lt. (jg) Robert Gibson found the cruiser flanked by *Wichita* and the light cruisers. After reporting her position, Gibson and wingman Ensign Russell Hoogerwerf

68   Stafford, 252-253.

turned away to locate the escort carriers. In their place, six Wildcats from the Big E's VF-10 set up CAP over TF 18.

By 3:45, eleven Japanese Bettys were reported south of New Georgia, heading toward Rennell Island. Despite vigilant CAP and fighter engagement, the Bettys headed north toward the *Chicago*. As the Bettys entered *Chicago*'s circle of escorts, additional Wildcats joined the fray, and along with vigorous anti-aircraft fire from the ships below, downed several Bettys. However, the well-trained enemy crews on the Bettys completed their mission. Despite a desperate, last-minute attempt by *Navajo* to turn *Chicago*'s bow to the attacker, four torpedoes slammed against the cruiser's already battered starboard side and detonated.

In moments it was clear *Chicago*'s fate was sealed, and she was ordered abandoned. At approximately 5:15, the cruiser rolled to starboard and slipped under the waves, stern first. *Chicago* was the last major American warship lost in the struggle for Guadalcanal. [69]

· ❧ ·

---

69   Steve Ewing. *USS Enterprise (CV-6): The Most Decorated Ship of World War II.* Missoula, MT.: Pictorial Histories Publishing Company, 1996, excerpt found at CV6. org entitled "USS Enterprise CV-6 The Most Decorated Ship of the Second World War: 1943" Rennell Island (January 29-30, 1943)," 5/22/2012 http://www.cv6.org/1943/ rennell/.

UNITED STATES NAVAL CHRONOLOGY WORLD WAR II

JANUARY 1943

29 FRI. Battle of Rennell Island (29-30 January) commences as cruiser and destroyer task force (Rear Adm. R. C. Giffen), covering movement of troop transports to Guadalcanal, Solomon Islands, is bombed near Rennell Island by Japanese aircraft.

30 SAT. Land and carrier-based naval aircraft engage Japanese aircraft attacking Rear Admiral Giffen's cruiser and destroyer force.

UNITED STATES NAVAL VESSEL SUNK:
- Heavy cruiser *Chicago* (CA-29), by aircraft torpedo

UNITED STATES NAVAL VESSEL DAMAGED:
- Destroyer *La Vallette* (DD-448), by aircraft torpedo

· ❁ ·

DITS AND DAHS, BUT NO DITCH

The *Enterprise* had plans to rendezvous with the new fleet arriving into the area, which included the *Saratoga*. The *Sara* was coming back into action. In those days the lack of communications meant both carrier groups maintained radio silence for fear of discovery by the Japanese. The ship asked for volunteers to search for the *Saratoga* and to drop a message on her deck giving the exact point to meet for the next morning. This was high-tech at its finest for those days.

The *Enterprise* captain wrote a message and put it in a bean bag for my delivery. I was instructed to drop my flaps and fly slowly across the deck of the carrier and drop the beanbag on the deck. I found the ship after making many detours because of large storm fronts on the search for about four hours. Therefore, I requested a position report from the *Saratoga* by a flashing lamp using Morse code to verify my navigation back to *Enterprise*. *Sara* sent back a position of fifteen degrees, so many minutes south latitude, the real location actually being at fourteen degrees. So, I plotted my course with faulty information.

Five in Morse code is five dits. Four is four dits and a dah. One dah represents sixty nautical miles. The error in flashing the code from *Saratoga* put me sixty miles south of the *Enterprise*. When I got to the point where the *Enterprise* was supposed to be, there was no ship. By this time, I was becoming quite concerned. After relying on the *Sara's* report there was only disaster ahead. Thereupon, I concentrated upon my plotting board, and fortunately surmised the problem instinctively. I realized there was no way that I could possibly get to land to ditch. We were at least 250 miles from any island, and I didn't have enough gas to get close enough to float in, so I knew it was either find the ship or it was the end of a wonderful life.

Once more, heightened awareness took over, and it once more saved my life. Heading due north for sixty miles, through the clouds I saw the fleet and the *Enterprise,* which had all planes spotted forward and was ready to take me aboard with less than five minutes of gas time left.

* ❀ *

BACK TO PEARL

In May 1943, the *Enterprise* set sail back to Pearl Harbor. This *Enterprise* cruise had left in October 1942, which meant that we had been gone for eight months. That was a fairly long period of time because America didn't have the necessary supply lines and repair facilities needed for longer periods. The US Navy shipping, however, was becoming increasingly stronger and the forward naval bases were becoming quite complex.

On our way into Pearl Harbor, we passed the *Essex* (CV-9). The first new carrier built since the War began and it was headed to the South Pacific. The *Enterprise* crew gave a loud cheer, to celebrate a new aircraft carrier joining in the fight to reach Tokyo. Large numbers of planes and replacement squadrons would soon be sent into the theater of battle. The tides of war had changed dramatically. America was on the move.

Prior to this time, replacement squadrons were concentrated in San Diego. Air Group 10, the last air group to come from the Pacific Coast, dated back to the previous September. It was almost eight months later before the Navy could send in a new air group. We didn't know it at the time, but from that point on there was going to be a huge onslaught of air group squadrons that would continuously push the Japanese back to their homeland.

No longer was the Japanese Imperial Navy the conqueror of all the sea. After November 1942, Japan could not again muster the staying power—or the willpower—to wage a strategic war with her navy. As brilliantly as Japan's navy had fought tactically in the surface and air engagements around Guadalcanal, once their veteran carrier air groups had been wiped out at the Battles of the Eastern Solomons and Santa Cruz, Japanese carriers ceased to be a strategic weapon.

· ❧ ·

THE CAMPAIGN CLOSES

The Guadalcanal campaign marked the turning point of the Pacific War. From that point forward, the initiative rested with the Allies. The vaunted Japanese forces were put into defensive mode. After six months of bitter fighting, Japan's last offensive operation in the Pacific had ended, finally, in defeat. "The cost of the campaign was staggering. For 2,500 square miles of jungle, tall grass, and sluggish rivers, the Allies had paid the cost of two fleet carriers, eight cruisers, fourteen destroyers, numerous smaller vessels and planes, and over 6,000 lives: nearly 1600 Marines and soldiers, the rest—there is still no exact figure—Navy officers and men. In their efforts to hold the island, Japan lost two battleships, a small carrier, four cruisers, eleven destroyers, and more than 23,000 men."[70] The Americans could replace their losses, as horrifying as they were. Japan, simply, could not.

· ❦ ·

HELL'S ISLAND

In the six-month fight over Guadalcanal, the two sides suffered roughly equivalent naval and air losses. Sixty-seven ships had been sunk—twenty-nine Allied, thirty-eight Japanese. The Japanese destroyed two American aircraft carriers and damaged a third carrier—the *Enterprise,* the sole remaining Allied carrier in the South Pacific. The Americans claimed two light aircraft carriers and two battleships. Both sides lost a sizable fleet of cruisers, destroyers, and noncombatant transports and cargo ships that could not be easily replaced.

"Each side lost between 600 and 700 aircraft in the campaign, but the fraction of downed aviators who were recovered told a different story. The Allies lost about 420 pilots and aircrew in the Solomons; the Japanese more than three times that number. Since the Battle of Coral Sea in May 1942, Japanese aircrew losses had consistently exceeded those of the Allies, often by a wide margin. Most striking was the disproportion in troop losses. The US Army and Marine Corps had suffered casualties of 5,875, of whom 1,592 were killed in action. The Japanese army had lost two full divisions on the island—14,700 killed or missing in action, and estimated 9,000 dead of starvation or disease, and more than 4,300 lost at sea while in transit to or from the island."[71]

· ❦ ·

---

70   Ewing, http://www.cv6.org/1943/rennell/.
71   Toll, *The Conquering Tide*, 187-188.

*TOTAL AND COMPLETE DEFEAT OF JAPANESE FORCES ON
GUADALCANAL EFFECTED 1625 TODAY. . . . AM HAPPY TO REPORT
THIS KIND OF COMPLIANCE WITH YOUR ORDERS. . . "TOKYO
EXPRESS" NO LONGER HAS TERMINUS ON GUADALCANAL.*

ORGANIZED RESISTANCE ON GUADALCANAL HAS CEASED.

—Feb 9, 1943 Dispatch—Maj. Gen. Alexander Patch
to Vice Adm. Halsey

"When Enterprise *slipped through the narrow channel past Fort
Kamehameha and Hospital Point and into bustling rebuilding Pearl,
it had been over nine months since she left. Nine months ago no one
had ever heard of an island Guadalcanal."[72]*

UNITED STATES NAVAL
CHRONOLOGY WORLD WAR II

FEBRUARY 1943

8 MON. Evacuation of over 11,000 Japanese troops from Guadalcanal,
Solomon Islands, is completed.

9 TUE. Organized resistance on Guadalcanal, Solomon Islands, ends. The
bitter struggle to capture Guadalcanal and other islands in the southern
Solomon Islands spanned 6 months and was the initial United States
offensive move in the Pacific War. It was extremely costly in men, ships, and
material, for both sides.

---

72   Stafford, 263.

USS *Enterprise* (CV-6) receives Presidential Unit Citation, May 27, 1943 (US Navy)

PRESIDENTIAL UNIT CITATION

DEC. 7, 1941–NOV. 15, 1942

On the morning May 27, 1943, Fleet Admiral Chester Nimitz boarded *Enterprise*. As the men in dress whites stood in orderly rows on the flight deck, Nimitz presented *Enterprise* and her men with a unit decoration: the first Presidential Unit Citation ever awarded to a carrier.

President Franklin Roosevelt authorized the Citation on February 6, 1943. It read:

For consistently outstanding performance and distinguished achievement during repeated action against enemy Japanese forces in the Pacific war area, December 7, 1941, to November 15, 1942. Participating in nearly every major carrier engagement in the first year of the war, the Enterprise and her air group, exclusive of far-flung destruction of hostile shore installations throughout the battle area, did sink or damage on her own a total of 35 Japanese vessels and shoot down a total of 185 Japanese aircraft. Her aggressive spirit and superb combat efficiency are fitting tribute to the officers and men who so gallantly established her as an ahead bulwark in the defense of the American nation. [73]

---

[73] "The Tokyo Raid was not mentioned because it was possible that the Japanese had still not figured out where Doolittle's B-25s had come from." Stafford, 265.

1942	ACTION AGAINST JAPAN'S FORCES	JAPANESE LOSSES		
		Ships Sunk	Ships Damaged	Planes Destroyed
FEB. 1	GILBERT AND MARSHALL ISLANDS RAID	8	* 4	36
FEB. 24	WAKE ISLAND RAID	1	*	3
MAR. 4	MARCUS ISLAND RAID		*	
APRIL 18	DOOLITTLE TOKYO RAID			
JUNE 4-6	BATTLE OF MIDWAY	2	4	9
AUG. 7-9	OCCUPATION OF GUADALCANAL		*	13
AUG. 24	BATTLE OF STEWART ISLANDS	1	1	44
OCT. 26	BATTLE OF SANTA CRUZ ISLANDS		3	63
NOV. 14-15	BATTLE OF SOLOMON ISLANDS	15	* 4	17
	(MINOR ENGAGEMENTS NOT INCLUDED) TOTAL	27	16	185
	* DESTRUCTIONS OF SHORE INSTALLATIONS			

DEC 7-1941 TO SEPT. 29.42	Enterprise Air Group VB-6 VF-6 VS-6 VT-6 VB-3 VS-5 VT-3
SEPT.30.42 TO NOV 15.42	AIR GROUP TEN VB-10 VF-10 VS-10 VT-10 VB-20

They will live a long time, these men of the South Pacific. They had an American quality. They, like their victories, will be remembered as long as our generation lives. After that, like the men of the Confederacy, they will become strangers. Longer and longer shadows will obscure them, until their Guadalcanal sounds distant on the ear like Shiloh and Valley Forge.

—James Michener, *Tales of the South Pacific*

STATESIDE

CHAPTER NINE

SHORE LEAVE AND WAR BONDS

Air Group Ten, San Francisco

*"Get ready to place the
jack under the axle and I will lift the car up."*

—Jack Dempsey

Enterprise Pilots Tell of Battles, *Chicago Sun*, **June 18, 1943**
(L to R): Lt. Leonard "Bud" Lucier, Lt. Robert Gibson, and Lt. Russell Hoogerwerf

ARRIVING AT PEARL Harbor, we staged a Second Battle of the Royal Hawaiian but avoided the shore patrol this time around. But we didn't avoid trouble, of course. Part of that concerned the reunion with my brother Roger, who had enlisted in the Navy and was on his way to the Philippines. I literally ran into him in Hawaii. After I sneaked him into our room at the Royal Hawaiian, it went downhill from there. We all had our allotment of whiskey and more and were raising hell. A hotel security guy gave us crap and we told him, "We've been out winning the fucking war, and what have you been doing?" He said, "Get the hell out of here." And we did.

From Pearl Harbor our air group was ordered to go to San Francisco. We embarked on a transport and seven days later arrived there. Meanwhile the war had changed its complexion entirely. The US had built up a huge backlog of naval pilots and ammunition, aircraft, and aircraft carriers. So, by the time I got back to the Pacific in late 1944, it was an entirely different war. Instead of Americans being able to field less than 100 pilots, one carrier, and a couple of cruisers and eight or ten destroyers, as in 1942, the next time I saw the Pacific fleet was in the Philippines, at Leyte Gulf.

As I flew there, I could see ships for 100 miles, as far as the eye could see. There were hundreds of aircraft carriers, cruisers, destroyers, battleships, supply ships, and transports. The first sight of about 500 ships at anchor in the harbor was just amazing to me. Up to that point I always operated under the belief that if I was killed, we would lose the war. It was quite a revelation to see this huge change that had transpired in less than two years.

It wasn't until we passed the brand-new Carrier No. 9, the *Essex*, the first of a magnificent new class of carriers, that we really knew there were any aircraft or pilots or air groups or ships being scheduled for the South Pacific. We blamed Roosevelt and others in Washington as well as Churchill and Stalin for diverting the vast majority of the war effort to Africa and Europe. The truth was, however, that Roosevelt was wisely using Russian soldiers to bear the brunt of ground and air action. Meanwhile, we were sucking hind teat in the Pacific.

We were glad to get out of the war zone in 1943 and into San Francisco and didn't know what modern life was like, so it was quite a shock. Equally amazing was to return to the Pacific in 1945 after spending a year and a half in the States and finding out what a tremendously changed war it was.

· ❧ ·

HOMEWARD BOUND

When we got aboard ship in Honolulu to go to San Francisco, a couple of fellows had wives in Pearl Harbor, and they came back with us. There was Jig Ramage, who became an admiral, and his wife Ti. I think she was part Hawaiian. Bernie Strong had also married a girl from Honolulu, who came back with our crowd as well.

The accommodations aboard ship were good and in seven days we had a lot of fun. Arriving in San Francisco for two weeks was also fun and games. We were met at the ship by the Gray Ladies of the American Red Cross and came ashore at the Naval Air Station at Alameda. These ladies picked us up in station wagons and drove us to the Fairmont Hotel, high on Nob Hill.

San Francisco in June of 1943 was the embarkation point for all the people crossing the Pacific Ocean. We—Air Group Ten—were the first actual air group to come back to the States intact. We had spent more time together in the war than any other air group and were involved in the most critical days of the war in the Pacific. The Battle of Midway was an incredible victory, but the critical battle was at Guadalcanal. At last, the momentum of war was going America's way but there was still a great austerity program on in the country. The speed limit was 45 mph, signs and posters all over the country said, "Is this trip necessary?" Plus, you had to get ration stamps for gas, for food, shoes, clothes, practically everything.

San Francisco was so exciting. The Fairmont Hotel was the *in* place where everything was happening. It was the Fairmont and the Mark

Hopkins across the street, the St. Francis and the Sir Francis Drake—
four great hotels for action. And San Francisco took our Air Group
Ten into their hearts every place we went.

This was during the height of the war, and everyone was wearing
uniforms, fully dressed according to regulations. They were practically
thrown in jail if they didn't have their tie two-blocked. Not so, Air
Group Ten. The shore patrol no doubt had been told to lay off this
wild group as we roamed the city non-regulation. And did we roam!

Speaking of out of uniform, sometime thereafter I was flying a plane
across country and when I landed to refuel, it was 100 plus degrees with
humidity hanging near 100 also there in Louisiana. A jack-assed Navy
captain came up and chewed me out. I thought, *Screw you, you bastard.*
I didn't have a tie on. I then climbed into my plane and took off leaving
the captain sweltering in the heat and a two-blocked necktie.

In San Francisco, we kept encountering the shore patrol. "Oh,
crap, we've met up with these bastards before," they said. I never had
a necktie on or coat or officer's insignia, and my left shoe still had a
hole cut out for my little toe. My shirtsleeves were torn, but this was
a badge of honor, and thus we roamed the streets, the best hotels, the
best restaurants, the most gorgeous girls in tow, and I looked like a
slob, except I was clean shaven and had my hair combed.

The air group was euphoric. America was not aware of what was
going on in the Pacific just as we were not aware of what was going
on in America! No one can understand war who hasn't been to war.
Just as no one can understand the heartaches and the sacrifice of
the people who have children at war until you have a child at war.
We didn't understand them, and they didn't understand us, but we
were all getting along pretty nicely. It was a great feeling to be in San
Francisco—every bar took care of us—*on the house,* most of the time.

The first night we were in town, some of our group roamed the
city streets together and invited every girl to come along. By the time
we got to the Top of the Mark, there were six or eight guys and thirty
girls. We expected to attract a ratio of four to one because the main
thing was to see all the girls possible in the world. We had parties in

our suites of rooms, too. In one dormitory-like room they had half a dozen beds. There were about ten of us in the room one day as we did handstands and somersaults, and one person flew out the window—it was hit the bed and bounce through the open window to the sidewalk five feet below. Others tried it, too, and some actually made it!

The Fairmont had built a room called the Kon-Tiki in which the hotel produced rainstorms with lightning and thunderstorms. There was an orchestra, dancing, and many girls acting as hostesses. Here was this sophisticated city of San Francisco with a tremendous influx of military personnel heading overseas to win the war, and here on the other hand were fifty to sixty guys who had come back from overseas who figured they had won the war and wanted to have a good time. We raised hell for about ten days before we went back to Alameda Naval Air Base to be assigned to our next station.

* 🍀 *

THE FIRST LINE

On June 17, 1943, Bud Lucier, Rod Hoogerwerf, and I were invited by J.P. Wrigley Company in Chicago to be featured on its weekly radio networked program called *The First Line*. The weekly program was aired by CBS through the Chicago affiliate WBBM. My appearance was on Episode 76 of the program that had been running for a year and half. The program was run live and required rehearsals each day starting on Monday through Thursday when it was aired.

The staff required for the program included "Jack Armstrong, the All-American Boy" and other actors of note in the Chicago area. As the one-hour story opened and closed, Bud, Red, and I had speaking parts, but as the story unfolded, Armstrong and the other professionals took over. A live orchestra provided the music, and operators of two giant turntables furnished the special sound effects, along with a conglomeration of devices such as washboards, combs, whistles, and horns.

I was also invited to meet "Old Field" (Marshall's father) in his office at the newspaper. This meeting helped me continue a long relationship with the Field family.

The First Line concentrated on the Navy, and that brought me into contact with the Public Relations Office of the Navy in Chicago. In every off moment the Navy PR contact kept us busy with interviews and other events. One event was called by Chicago's political boss, Mayor Ed Kelly, who staged a noon-time expo in front of City Hall, complete with press reviews, dignitaries, a band, radio, cameras, flash bulbs, and an audience of thousands standing in front of our platform erected for the occasion. It was then that I particularly became aware of someone who was always grabbing my elbow and directing me where to go, to stand, what to say, pushing me through a door into a room or into a car, watching the minute hand on a watch, and making me do yet another interview retelling the same baloney.

One night I spoke to 5,000 WAVES, women's auxiliary volunteers, who were joining the Navy that night. I especially liked that event. However, as the week progressed, I became increasingly peeved at the PR people always guiding me around by the elbow.

They asked me to let them handle a two-month publicity tour nationwide. I got the feeling that I was a trained monkey and that it wasn't right for me to be doing this when so many of my friends had died. Plus, the tugging on my elbow was annoying me.

The Wrigley Company had provided me with a suite of rooms at the Ambassador East Hotel, and the Navy told me I was to have an interview with *Time* and *Life* magazines at 9 a.m. on Friday right after the broadcast the night before. There was a chance I'd get a cover story from this. PR would also give me my itinerary for the next two months at that morning meeting.

Everything considered, and because of my feeling for departed comrades, I realized that for two months I would be cashing in on being alive while Durkin, Jackard, Chaffee, Dexter, Goddard, and all the others, now dead, were left out. I decided to duck out.

I checked out of the Ambassador East at 8 a.m. Friday, June 18, 1943, one hour before the interview, without warning the Navy PR people or *Time* or *Life* and headed on the road to my assignment in Texas.

Although I booted the chance for self-aggrandizement in the form of promoting myself on a personal tour and appearances, I later participated in several War Loan fund raisers. Fundraising programs always included spotlighting several celebrities to draw crowds and the single purpose was to raise financing to buy more planes and to train more pilots. These occasions fit within my comfort zone.

Sometimes I have thought how my life would have been changed by that Friday morning interview and the two-month campaign. I then wonder if I did the right thing in passing up the fame. The publicity might have led me to accept Clare Magee's offer to get into politics.

On second thought, taking a look at any TV news program today and what comes with notoriety, I say "Hooray for being an Average American." It was a good decision.

· ✤ ·

WAR BONDS

The War Finance Committee in charge of loan drives sold a total of $185.7 billion of securities. The enormity of this effort can best be realized as equal to $6 trillion in 2020 values. This incredible mass-selling achievement to help finance the war has not been matched before or since. By the end of the war, over eighty-five million Americans had invested in War Bonds, a number unmatched by any other country. The fifteen billion dollar goal of the Third War Loan[74] meant that the record amount of bonds sold in a single month would have to be doubled, meaning that over forty million of America's 130 million citizens would have to invest in a $100 Series E

---

74   The First War Loan ($13 billion), timed with the US victory at Guadalcanal, began on November 30, 1942 and ended December 23, 1942. The Second War Loan ($18.5 billion) was launched on April 12, 1943 and completed May 1, 1943. The three war loans in 1942 and 1943 generated nearly $1 trillion in sales in today's dollars.

Savings Bond. Over 107 percent of the individual sales quota was reached, and the Third War Loan's final sales totaled almost nineteen billion dollars.

• ✿ •

HEAVYWEIGHTS

On September 16, 1943, I participated in a Third War Loan program in Fort Worth, Texas, an affair that was held at the Will Rogers Memorial Auditorium. The program scheduled me to speak in between actor William Holden and heavy-weight champion Jack Dempsey.

Earlier in the day, I flew my plane into the Naval Air Station at Grand Prairie, Texas, for two reasons: it was the closest Navy field to Fort Worth, and I was to rendezvous there with Jack Dempsey, the prize fighter. Dempsey was serving in the Coast Guard as a lieutenant commander, and I planned my arrival to coincide with his.

A Navy automobile with driver was scheduled to drive us the twenty miles or so to Fort Worth. On the way we experienced what was a common occurrence in those days, a flat tire. Added to the inconvenience, we found that the car jack would not function properly, whereupon Dempsey said, "Get ready to place the jack under the axle and I will lift the car up." He did, and the tire change went smoothly.

Jack Dempsey was one of America's first great sports heroes. His savage style captivated the public and made him as popular a figure as Babe Ruth or Red Grange. In the ring, Dempsey used a two-fisted attack. He boxed out of a low crouch, bobbing, weaving, and bombing. He continually stalked the man in front of him and was an unrelenting, remorseless warrior. His power was so prodigious that he once scored knockouts in fourteen and eighteen seconds. In his seventy-eight-bout career, Dempsey compiled forty-nine knockouts with twenty-five of them in the first round.

A reliable and boyishly handsome leading man in the 1940s Hollywood, William Holden made an acclaimed breakthrough in the 1950s *Sunset Boulevard* as a jaded screenwriter who plays a gigolo to faded leading lady Gloria Swanson. Holden was the premier leading man of the late '50s, often starring in gritty, all-male war dramas, winning an Oscar for *Stalag 17,* and playing opposite the decade's greatest leading ladies—Grace Kelly, Audrey Hepburn, Kim Novak, and Jennifer Jones.

And on that September night in 1943, I was wedged in between them. It was some celebration.

· ✦ ·

New Skipper of Squadron 14-A, Kingsville Naval Air Station, Texas, September 1944

Lyndon Johnson came from the hill country west of Austin, Texas, but I met him at his home in Austin. The occasion was yet another Third War Bond Loan program to be performed before 30,000 that night in the football stadium at the University of Texas. I was picked up after landing at Bergstrom Field and delivered to my hotel for check-in prior to being taken to Johnson's home. Johnson was a US congressman at the time. I thought about my own hometown congressman Clare Magee, who had been elected shortly after murdering his cousin in broad daylight on my hometown square in Unionville, Missouri. Both men had similar backgrounds, having come from hilly US regions with hard-scrabble roots. Cocktails and dinner were served at Johnson's home, after which our group departed by motorcade with dozens of motorcycle police and sirens blaring, to the University of Texas stadium.

· ✦ ·

Despite these moments of some fame, I had work to do. The war continued, as did I.

CHAPTER TEN

TEXAS HOLD'EM

"You get to select the one you want!"

Hoot Gibson glamour shot for War Bonds tour 1943

CORPUS CHRISTI

I WAS ASSIGNED to pilot training at the air station at Waldron Field, Naval Air Station Corpus Christi, Texas as the executive officer of Training Squadron 16B there. Bud Lucier and John Boudreaux were also assigned to Corpus Christi. Later, I went to Kingsville, where I was commanding officer of Training Squadron 14A. As CO, I had a hundred and some aircraft at Kingsville. The squadron taught pilots to become ready for flying on carriers, and overall, I probably graduated 1,500 cadets from SNJs.[75]

· ✤ ·

Mass-producing pilots to match the thousands—24,000 in 1944 alone—of new combat aircraft assembled by American manufacturers was a challenge. The Navy awarded 20,842 and 21,067 "wings of gold," respectively, in 1943 and 1944. They did this without compromising training standards. Indeed, the rookie crop of 1944 arrived in frontline squadrons with an average of six hundred flight hours, including two hundred hours in the service planes to which they were assigned. This feat was made possible by the expansion of the main training complex at Pensacola, Florida, and the establishment of twelve new naval air stations around the country, including the Air Stations at Corpus Christi and Kingsville, Texas.

Throughout the daylight hours and often at night, the skies above were crowded with low-flying airplanes. Fatal accidents were unexceptional, and empty pine coffins were stored in stacks along the walls of the hangers. At the height of the war, there was an average of one crash per day at Pensacola."[76]

---

75   The SNJ (Scout Trainer North American) was the Navy's designation of the advanced trainer manufactured by North American Aviation. The Army designated it the AT-6 ("Texans").

76   Toll, *Twilight of the Gods*, 420.

Most squadron leaders, like Hoot, were veterans of carrier operations in the Pacific. They knew the challenges the rookies would face when deployed, so they taught lots of formation tactics and air-to-air and air-to-ground gunnery, instrument and night flying, and dog fighting.

The young pilots often broke regulations, sometimes with the tacit approval of their leaders. "Flathatting"— flying very low to the ground—was prohibited by standing regulations, especially in populated civilian areas. But in wartime, especially, many aviators flouted the prohibition. Navy planes flying from NAS Corpus Christi flew low over the nearby King Ranch, driving herds of cattle, while the cowboys shook their fists.[77]

· ❧ ·

COPACABANA

While in Corpus Christi, I was asked to ferry a twin-engine Beechcraft to Quonset Point, Rhode Island. Today, this is normally a day and a half to get there and a half-day to return. Not so in 1944! As I was sitting in the airplane revving up for takeoff, the tower gave me final clearance to proceed on instruments to Barksdale Air Force Base in Louisiana for refueling. However, before reaching liftoff, the weather socked in and the rest of the flight was strictly on instruments. As I cleared the road at the far end of the runway, three of my friends were driving under my plane. They commented, "Wonder who that damn fool is?" They didn't know it was me, and I didn't know that the car was theirs, but the event signaled once again the hazards of flying in those days, albeit it's pretty routine today.

Recounting this trip also sheds more light on life in the US during the War. Along for the ride, taking them as far as Atlanta, was Harry Seay, the engineering officer in my squadron, and a flight surgeon from the base.

77　Toll, *Twilight of the Gods*, 423-424.

Leaving Barksdale the next morning, the weather was great and the journey to Atlanta passed without event. The following morning was an entirely different story, weather wise, though, as a snowstorm closed in north of takeoff and continued all the way to Washington DC, where I was to land at Anacostia Naval Air Station. Instrument flying in those days left a lot to be desired as pilots had access to a radio beam, but little other help other than flying with the needle-ball-airspeed indicators, the compass, and a clock. Occupying the hands of the pilot was usually the stick, or wheel, in one hand, while the other sweaty palm clutched an aviation map. I was all alone, a dive-bomber pilot, stupid enough to be flying a twin-engine plane I had never flown before, and in one hell of a snowstorm socked in clear to the ground.

A common statement by my ilk was, "I can fly the crates the airplanes come in." Up there, I had time to ruminate upon that subject. As I approached the Washington area, I had two choices. Either divert or drop to treetop level and punch my way through as there was no such thing as an instrument landing in my world. And even if there had been, my self-confidence as a pilot exceeded my belief in what was not even known then as *electronics*. I figured the fog and snow were at ground level, and thus a standard-procedure let-down by radio would not work.

I estimated the time that I would break through in a descent that would put me over the Chesapeake Bay and started descending. At about fifty feet, I broke through but was over water. No trees or towers to worry about. Just keep flying on course up the Bay and do a lot of praying. The Anacostia Field and its main runway was immediately adjacent to the east edge of the Bay. Hugging the water for a period of twenty minutes or so brought me within a few feet of the runway, and then straight in for a landing.

It snowed for one solid week. All flights in and out of Washington were grounded. I spent the week living on the per diem that the Navy paid me. That was the magnificent sum of seven dollars per day, representing hotel and meals for each day. Try that today!

This epic flight took off again after shoveling off one week's supply of snow on the plane's wings and clear skies that led me into the Naval Air Station, Quonset Point, Rhode Island. As a ferry pilot, for the moment I had been issued a number two air priority for getting on commercial flights. Only the big shots in Washington rated the higher number one priority. The ferry pilot could bounce any other passenger and did as the movement of planes to embarkation ports was vital overseas.

Immediately after landing, I proceeded to Eastern Airlines and caught a flight to LaGuardia Airport at New York, arriving there about 2 p.m. The next plane left at midnight going to Chicago Midway Airport with these stops: Harrisburg, Pittsburgh, Columbus, Dayton, and Indianapolis. Then on into Midway. The airliner flew at 5,000 feet in violent thunderstorms and each leg of the trip was very rough.

Before leaving New York, I took a taxi into Manhattan and found myself having a cocktail at the small bar in the Pierre Hotel. It was after 5 p.m. when a man stopped by for a martini before proceeding home. He was friendly and could see from my conversation that I was at loose ends until my flight at midnight. Before he left, he asked the bartender for the phone, made a quick call and told me he had arranged for my dinner for the evening. His name was DeYoung and he came from San Francisco. I recognized his name as a pioneer family there, and so I accepted his gracious offer. Whereupon he hailed a taxi, put me in it, and gave instructions to the driver.

My cab pulled up in front of the Copacabana Club to let me out. Standing there at the curb was the owner of the club, who told me that he was the person DeYoung had called and that my evening was paid for. It was now dark and into the dinner hour. The owner said, "I am excusing one of the chorus girls to have dinner with you and you get to select the one you want," as he led me to the dressing room. This is the God's honest truth. It is not a joke or a fairy tale even though it sounds like the answer to every man's dreams. The owner then asked for my selection of one of perhaps twenty, and I had my dinner date. We sat at the bar for a few minutes, when the owner returned, saying, "Your booth is ready, and you will be joined for dinner by our headliner, after which you will see his show." Arriving at the booth, you can imagine my surprise to see Jimmy Durante standing there. Sure enough, we had dinner! I saw Durante's show, and the owner put me in a cab for the trip back to the airport. What a treat for a young buck in a uniform with a ribbon. What are the chances of that happening today?

After six landings to get from New York to Chicago, we flew the remaining part of the night, arriving at Midway about noon. Flights again were curtailed because of weather, the terminal was overflowing, and people were sitting on the floor. And a number two priority had no power to get any plane into the storm-swept skies. The clock ticked on, as the night passed with no place to sit or stand, and finally at dawn the first plane was heading to Texas, and I was on it. Then came landing at Davenport, Des Moines, Kansas City, Wichita, Tulsa, Oklahoma City, Dallas, San Antonio, and finally Corpus Christi. It felt like the arrival was sometime the next week. Another little picture of life in wartime America.

· ❈ ·

PARACHUTES

At the Naval Air Station in Kingsville, the base commander kept his plane and parachute in my squadron. He was violently hated by all hands, though. Inadvertently one day, I discovered that the base commander's parachute was stuffed with old rags instead of a chute. As one of my old friends and an ace pilot on the *Enterprise* said, it is important to know who is packing your parachute. Everyone has someone who provides what they need to make it through the day. Sometimes in the daily challenges that life gives us, we miss what is really important. And it is important to recognize the people who pack your parachute.

· ❈ ·

TIME TO BOLT

Late summer 1943 the Truman Committee visited the North American Aircraft and the Southern Aircraft plants near Dallas. The committee reported widespread dissatisfaction with the work product at both plants that resulted in a tremendous amount of bad publicity appearing in the nation's press. Thousands of workers went home at night facing criticism from their neighbors as a result. Morale kept diving at the plants and production efforts suffered as well. Meanwhile production of P-51s was hitting the skids.

The aircraft plants were in Grand Prairie, about half-way between Dallas and Fort Worth. The Navy had a naval air station located there also.

In October 1943, the Office of Inspector of Naval Material, Navy Department, requested that Bud Lucier and I, as Navy fliers with war experience, be assigned temporary duty in Dallas for the express purpose of counteracting the negative effect brought about by the Truman Committee. For two weeks, Bud and I gave pep talks to small groups of 50 to 2,000 employees at the two facilities. Both of us had flown North American planes and knew their excellent features, and so we could speak with authority.

Bud Lucier would tell a funny story to the group. In his hometown of Davenport, Iowa, when he worked for John Deere Tractor across the Mississippi River in Moline, Illinois, his job was to tighten the bolt that held the tractor driver's seat up.

Later, when he found himself diving on a Japanese ship, as he started to pull out, the bolt holding his seat in place failed, so he was pulling out of a dive with his seat so low he couldn't see out of the cockpit. Bud concluded, "I'm here to find which one of you forgot to tighten the seat." The story was a lighthearted entry into a stressful situation and won every worker over as a friend. We then explained our high regard for all North American planes, their easy operation and reliability, and our assurance that the employees there were doing a superb job.

. ✿ .

AMERICAN INDUSTRIAL MIGHT

American workers mobilized on a grand scale during the war. During the first three critical years following Pearl Harbor, Americans built 24 fleet aircraft carriers, 100 escort carriers, 8 battleships, 34 cruisers, 293 destroyers, 503 destroyer escorts, 167 submarines, 2,489 patrol and mine craft, 1,117 auxiliaries, and a remarkable 68,737 landing craft.[78] Times had changed since the shoestring naval force available for first year of the war. Simply put, the US Navy became overpowering.

---

78   Bureau of Naval Personnel, Information Bulletin, February 1945.

SECOND TOUR

CHAPTER ELEVEN

BORNEO AND BACK

Amphibious Group 8

On the beach—Manus Islands, New Guinea
(Hoot, is the quiet one, fourth from left)

THE WARPATH TO TOKYO

THE AUGUST 1942 to February 1943 Guadalcanal campaign marked the Allies' transition from defensive to offensive operations and effectively seized the strategic initiative in the Pacific theater from the Japanese.

While General MacArthur's Southwest Pacific land forces wore down the Japanese in New Guinea, the US Navy rebuilt, reconfigured, trained, and prepared a fleet capable of striking directly at the Japanese defensive ring and ultimately at its homeland through a Central Pacific offensive thrust. To accomplish this, Admiral Nimitz, Pacific Fleet commander, organized the Central Pacific Force—later named the Fifth Fleet—under the command of Admiral Raymond Spruance with a Fast Carrier Force (Task Force 58), a Joint Expeditionary Force (Task Force 51), and an Expeditionary Force (Task Force 56). Admiral Spruance and Admiral Bull Halsey alternated command of the Central Pacific Fleet every six months to the end of the war. Curiously, the massive Central Pacific force became the Third Fleet and Task Force 38 when Admiral Halsey was in command and then renamed back to the Fifth Fleet and Task Force 58 when Admiral Spruance returned to command. This hand-off system of fleet commanders and commands continued back and forth until the end of the war. Instead of changing horses, they changed riders.

Following a bloody fight in November 1943 on Tarawa, the US Navy in the Central Pacific struck a series of islands in the Gilbert and Marshall Islands throughout 1944, including at Kwajalein, Eniwetok, and Truk in February. The offensive campaign continued into the Mariana and Palau Islands, including on Saipan, Tinian, Guam, and the Philippines Sea from June to July and Peleliu from September to November. To the southwest, General MacArthur and his South West Pacific forces were slugging northward from Australia through New Guinea in the Dutch East Indies—now Indonesia—in a tough Hollandia-Aitape campaign, while bypassing several Japanese-held island ports and strongholds on its heading toward a return to the Philippines in late 1944, early 1945. Meanwhile, as we know, Hoot was stateside from late 1943 to late 1944 training hundreds of new carrier pilots at Corpus Christi and Kingsville Navy Airfields for the carrier fleet in the grand finale push toward the Japanese mainland.

Hard and bloody campaigns remained to be fought against determined Japanese forces when Hoot returned to the Pacific as the air officer for

Amphibious Group 8 in late 1944. Multiple campaigns remained from late 1944 to the end of the war, including the Philippines campaign at Leyte, Luzon and the rest of the Philippine islands, and the Bonin and Ryuku Islands campaign at Iwo Jima and Okinawa respectively, from February through June 1945.

And there was Borneo. The Borneo campaign was the last major Allied campaign in the South West Pacific Area during the war. Its objective was to liberate Japanese-held British Borneo and Dutch Borneo. Designated collectively as Operation Oboe, a series of amphibious assaults between May 1 and July 21 were conducted by the Australian I Corps against Imperial Japanese forces who had been occupying the island since early 1942. The Australian ground forces were supported by US and other Allied air and naval forces, with the US providing the bulk of the shipping and logistic support necessary to conduct the operation. Landings were undertaken at four locations: Tarakan, Labuan, North Borneo, and Balikpapan. While major combat operations were concluded by mid-July, mopping-up operations continued throughout Borneo in August.

Then the atomic bombs—Little Boy and Fat Man—destroyed Hiroshima and Nagasaki, forcing Japan to reconsider its plan to fight to the death. Japan surrendered. The Pacific war was over.

· ❧ ·

SECOND TOUR

At the end of 1944, I was sent back overseas as the air officer on the staff of Rear Admirals William Fechteler and Arthur Noble, commanders of Amphibious Group 8 of the Seventh Amphibious Force under Vice Admiral Daniel Barbey. As air officer, I was involved in the planning and overseeing of landing operations in the Philippines and Borneo through the end of the war. Amphibious Group 8 was very busy.

· ❧ ·

The Command History of the Seventh Amphibious Force details the vital battles and operations conducted while Hoot was assigned to Amphibious Group 8.

Capture of the Philippines
October 1944—February 1945

From the beginning, the Commander, Seventh Amphibious Force, utilized one naval aviator on his staff for air planning, as air advisor, and as liaison with participating units of the Far East Air Forces and Allied Air Force and with Carrier units of the Pacific Fleet.

The amphibious landings at Leyte, Philippine Islands, were made on 20 October 1944. The Seventh Fleet was in overall command of the ships engaged in the Leyte Operation which included Amphibious Group 8. They landed the XXIV Army Corps on the southern beaches in the vicinity of Dulag; and Lieutenant General Walter Kreuger, Commanding General, Sixth Army, was responsible for securing Leyte and the adjacent island of Samar. The amphibious landings were eminently successful, but the supporting ships suffered from suicide air attacks, effectively employed against our naval forces for the first time.

Thereafter, the amphibious operations of the Seventh Amphibious Force assumed a new pattern to meet the need for simultaneous operations for the earliest control of the entire Philippine Archipelago. Individual operations were placed under the command of the amphibious group commanders. These consolidating operations took place in late January 1945 and included the Amphibious Group 8 landing of the 11th Airborne Division at Nasugbu, south of Manila Bay which assisted materially in the capture of the Capital.

Consolidating Operations in the Philippines and Borneo
February 1945—July 1945

While fighting on Luzon was still in progress, the campaign for the recapture of the remaining islands in the Philippines and for the control of Borneo and the Netherlands East Indies was begun. Between February and May 1945, more than sixteen landing operations were conducted in the Central and Southern Philippines, and three major operations on the east and west coasts of Borneo.

The first in the series was the landing of a regimental combat team of the 40th Infantry Division at Puerta Princessa in the Palawan Island by Amphibious Group 8 on 28 February 1945. When Puerta Princessa was secured, air bases were established that enabled the air force to gain control over the China Sea.

On 17 April 1945, Rear Admiral Noble, who had succeeded Rear Admiral Fechteler as Commander Amphibious Group 8, directed a two-division landing by the X Corps at Parang and Malabang in the Cotabato area of Mindanao. The landing areas had previously been secured by guerrillas, so troops moved quickly overland and captured Davao. Meanwhile, naval support forces moved into Davao Gulf and destroyed suicide boats, midget submarines, and their bases. Elements of the X Corps moved northward from Davao and met increasing Japanese resistance in the mountainous part of Central Mindanao. On 1 June 1945, Amphibious Group 8 withdrew to prepare for the Balikpapan operation.

Owing to the importance of preparation for the invasion of Japan, plans for control of the Netherlands East Indies were restricted to the capture of strategic areas in Dutch and British Borneo. The final amphibious assault landing in Borneo was made on 1 July 1945 at Balikpapan. Vice Admiral Barbey was in overall command of this operation with the

Amphibious Group 8 directly responsible for landing the 7th Australian Division.

Although it was not realized at the time, the Balikpapan operation was the last for the Seventh Amphibious Force and Amphibious Group 8, which had completed a two-year combat record of 56 amphibious assault landings involving overwater movement of a total of more than a million men. During July and August 1945, ships of the Seventh Amphibious Force were engaged in redistributing Army Units and preparing plans for the final assault on the Japanese homeland.[79]

· ❀ ·

ENOUGH

So we made a couple of landings in the Philippines and four more thereafter in the East Indies, and a last one in Borneo. During this second Pacific tour, I served in the Leyte Gulf, Tacloban, Samar, Mindanao, and Luzon in the Philippines during the liberation from the Japanese, and I served in Indonesia at Manus, New Guinea, Celebes, Morotai, as well as in Balikpapan, Borneo, for the last invasion of the war. I was in thirteen battles by the time it was all over, and in thirteen more bad situations, not coinciding with those battles, but facing operational situations and battles where I was a split-second away from disaster.

The war was over, and I decided to hang up my wings. I got out in October 1945. I had plenty of points. We were in Manila heading for Tokyo when I said to the admiral, "I'm going home. Here are my orders. I've had them typed and all I need is to have you sign them."

"Okay," he said, and signed them.

I jumped onto the harbor pilot-boat, as our ship was leaving Manila harbor and hitch-hiked my way back across the Pacific to San Francisco, where I separated from the service. My war was done.

---

79   Seventh Amphibious Force, Command History, Naval History and Heritage Command.

UNITED STATES NAVAL CHRONOLOGY WORLD WAR II

AUGUST 1945

14 TUE. Japan accepts the provisions of the Potsdam Declaration and agrees to surrender. General of the Army Douglas MacArthur, USA, is named Supreme Allied Commander to receive the Japanese capitulation and conduct the occupation of Japan.

UNITED STATES NAVAL CHRONOLOGY WORLD WAR II

SEPTEMBER 1945

2 SUN. Japanese surrender documents are signed on board the battleship *Missouri* (BB-63) at anchor in Tokyo Bay, Japan. General of the Army Douglas MacArthur signs for the Allied Powers, and Fleet Adm. C. W. Nimitz signs for the United States.

CHAPTER TWELVE

MISSOURI TO MISSOURI: AFTERTHOUGHTS

*"In that time bold commissioning-day promises to sail into harm's
way acquired human and material consequences.
This was naval warfare in the machine age."[80]*

Japanese *Kinigawa Maru* beached on Guadalcanal,
November 1942 (US Navy)

---

80   James D. Hornfischer, *The Last Stand of the Tin Can Sailors*, New York: Bantam, 2004, 206.

DAUNTLESS IN THE PACIFIC

"THE TWISTED METAL of the rusted hulk of the *Kinugawa Maru* bears testimony to the destructive force of the thousand-pound bomb dropped by SBD pilot Hoot Gibson on November 15, 1942. Violent surface duels between warships, two carrier conflicts, multi-day land battles, and daily aerial engagements failed to hand Guadalcanal over to the Imperial Japanese military. . . . The rusting hulk of *Kinugawa* is one of the few remaining pieces of visual evidence of the mid-November climax that determined the fate of Hell's Island [Guadalcanal]. This ghost ship is testimony to the hard-fought victory achieved in large part by the valiant young men like Gibson who once flew Dauntless dive-bombers from a dusty coral airstrip in the most trying of times."[81]

· ❀ ·

THE TURNING POINT

"Until then the Japanese had been advancing at their will. From then on the Japanese retreated at our will."

—Admiral Halsey

Both the American and Japanese navies were scared to death of each other. On occasion, admirals such as Dan Callaghan and Bull Halsey flung their units into *devil-take-the-hindmost* charges, but they were the exception. During the Guadalcanal Invasion and the three major defensive actions, both the American and Japanese admirals turned tail 180 degrees without following up in battle.

Every time the enemy hit us, they would have been smart to keep coming because our fleets were doing thirty-four knots hightailing it back the other way. They could have come in and polished us off. But,

---

81   Moore, *Hell's Island*, 427.

on the other hand they had a high attrition rate of pilots. The story being circulated amongst the American pilots was that the Japanese had no more than 100 first-line pilots still alive, and once they were gone, American could shoot down the replacement flyers with impunity. We would control the skies and our surface vessels would rule the seas.

Midway was not the turning point, nor did we have superiority over the Japanese after Midway. We didn't get air superiority until November 1942 after the Third Defense of Guadalcanal. Until then, after the remaining 100 first-line Japanese pilots were killed, the enemy was still dominant. During the daily grind of air action at Guadalcanal for three-plus months and two carrier battles in that area, the enemy's inventory of first-line pilots was savaged. Meanwhile, the Japanese had been unable to train such qualified pilots for replacement. Starting with Midway, our opponent had an estimated 400 good, smart, and aggressive pilots who were worthy opponents. After Midway and Guadalcanal, a handful.

In one sense it is difficult to understand how America ever won the war. Starting with watching Admiral Fletcher leave the *Yorktown* at Midway, I was then present at the Invasion of Guadalcanal when Fletcher again abandoned Turner and the invasion fleet. Other admirals pulled equally questionable actions under the guise of lack of fuel, lack of communications, or the protection of a carrier.

Add to the real problems of war the manic egos of admirals and generals, interservice power plays such as MacArthur and his successful attempts to hinder the Navy and his insistence on delaying victory by retaking the Philippines, a year and a half was lost, along with thousands of unnecessary American casualties and tons of equipment and supplies. Legend has it that Nimitz kept a picture of MacArthur prominently displayed in his office. It was an unsigned rotogravure clipped from a magazine. When asked about the general's perpetual presence, Nimitz gave one of his smiles and answered, "I'll tell you. It is to remind me not to be a horse's ass."[82]

---

82   Attributed in Rear Adm. Edward T. Layton's, *"And I Was There," Pearl Harbor and Midway—Breaking the Secrets*, New York: William Morrow, 1985, 484.

· ❦ ·

"THE JAP KILLER"

On takeoff, I was always amused when an officer was instructed to stand by my plane with a blackboard and these well-intentioned instructions, "Go get them. We'll be waiting for you when you come back." Meaning, "if you come back." So, in the eyes of the carrier seaman, carrier pilots could do no wrong. The most fearful fate in naval warfare is to be aboard a carrier while under attack. Rest assured if there are eighty enemy planes, one carrier, and ten supporting vessels, there will be eighty enemy planes attacking one ship alone—the carrier.

I figured I could take anything the Navy tossed at me, and also anything the Japanese threw my way. I gladly accepted the responsibility of killing Japanese before they could get to us for the same purpose. I had not forgotten my experience on the *Yorktown*, helpless through two attacks. This was, after all, war. It wasn't a game, and I was a highly trained killer for the safety of the United States. Even today, one admiral refers to me in an introduction as *the Jap killer*. That was one thing, as it turned out, that I was good at. That admiral was also very good at the same task.

· ❦ ·

THE JAPANESE ACE

Sakai was credited with shooting down sixty-four planes but he was honest enough to say he didn't have a count. Sakai could also have shot down many Russian fighters that had been used by the Chinese, but Japanese propaganda tried to indicate all kills as being American. That was simply impossible. From my experience in the war, at that early date, there was no way sixty-four American carrier planes had been shot down by any one man, nor by the entire Japanese Navy, for that matter. The majority of America's airplane losses came from operational factors, not from enemy air fire.

The Japanese had been fighting for a long time in China and they shot down a lot of kites over there and called them planes. The Zero was so light that two men could pick up a wing section. Powerfully armed and highly maneuverable, it had shot down many Russian-built 1-15 fighters of the Chinese Nationalists.

However, air action against the Japanese proved how wrong the assumptions were in Washington before the war that Japanese pilots could not fly and shoot straight because of their supposedly weak eyes. Avoiding such blind thinking might have dispelled such racial illusions and also have had a far-reaching effect on our state of preparedness three years later.

· ❀ ·

HEADHUNTERS

In 1942, all carrier pilots were informed of areas in the Guadalcanal and New Hebrides areas where it was rumored that head-hunting and cannibalism were currently being practiced. All pilots took these admonitions seriously, and we knew of the extreme danger we faced from falling into the hands of the Japanese with their brutal tactics. We had heard rumors about one of our pilots who was shot down at Midway and picked up by a Japanese destroyer. The captors spread-eagled the pilot on the deck and then took their time in hacking off his head. And then they threw the body overboard to feed the sharks.

As a result, we were all aware of the grisly fate of falling into the hands of the Japanese. Falling into the hands of headhunters was also not recommended. All crewmen carried a .45- or .38-caliber handgun, and I for one practiced shooting often by tacking a playing card onto a coconut tree in the jungle and having at it. I could make a pattern on the card from a respectable distance. And I hadn't forgotten the flying squirrels, either.

Such pilot caution was well illustrated on one occasion. A flight of six SBDs from Scouting Ten on the *Enterprise* found themselves lost in a storm far from the carrier. Running low on gas, they made a formation landing in the ocean very near a beach of an island considered unsafe because of the natives. Each rearseatman was instructed to remove the twin .30-caliber machine guns to be carried in each life raft, which they did. The pilots knew there were no Japanese on the island, however, they paddled to shore with twelve machine guns ready to fire.

Luckily, the natives were impressed with the evident firepower and received the crews as friends. The twelve men stayed at the village until they were rescued by a PBY. The news of the rescue was hailed on board the *Enterprise* and many hands were on spot to welcome them back aboard. But then we got a real shock, as each man came aboard carrying a human head on a stick. Their story went like this:

The natives who hosted them were led by a chief who was having difficulties, and that lead to his having his head chopped off. In retaliation, the dead chief's wife swore vengeance. She would invite the bad guys over to tea and then have their heads cut off, pickled in some manner and stuck on a stick to hang on the walls of her hut. In an act of friendliness, she made the gifts of the heads to our men. Captain Cook, who discovered the Tonga Islands, called them the Friendly Islands because of the people's friendliness. This island that the boys ditched their planes near could not be defined as friendly, at all times, however. The natives also had some secret process that enabled them to shrink a head while retaining all the physical features. Those heads were sort of fascinating in an odd way.

· ✤ ·

BANZAI BOOGIE

Facing murderous Japanese who had no regard for surrender, leading to their Banzai charges, caused me to name my airplane the *Banzai Boogie*. Statistics showed that the average number of prisoners taken by Americans was one out of one hundred fanatical Japanese, the rest refusing to surrender and being killed. The average for most other nations was one surrender for four dead. Banzai ruled and each man who was killed was believed to become one of the stars in the heavens. It gives one a little pause to understand what might have happened without the two atomic bombs being dropped.

Conversations with the natives were conducted with what we called *pidgin* English. They explained, and showed, their bayonet wounds to the Americans and told how the Japanese had bound natives to coconut trees and used them for bayonet practice. That also certainly gave me cause to stop and think.

* 🍁 *

BULLDOZER VICTORY

How did America end up winning the war? A hell of a lot of grit and luck, and then we also out-produced the Japanese. We could have killed the population of Japan with bulldozers, but it would have cost Japan millions of lives, considering their pact with the emperor to commit national suicide. At the end of the war, I saw tens of thousands of bulldozers on Guam. Workers were charged with getting rid of them and were chopping holes in the planes with axes to make certain they sank when dropped into the ocean. Bulldozers don't need to be chopped to ensure that they rest on the bottom of the sea.

* 🍁 *

THE SBD "DAUNTLESS"

Span: 41 feet, 6 inches.
Length: 33 feet.
Service Ceiling: 25,000 feet.

Approximate Maximum Speed: 245 miles per hour.

The SBD "Dauntless" was scheduled for phase out a year before Pearl Harbor, but it was pressed into the famous battles of Coral Sea, Midway, and Solomons, despite only a mediocre bomb load and range. She was capable far beyond her designed role. More than any other carrier airplane of World War II, the SBD became a classic. It flew like a fighter and took punishment like a B-17. Providentially, it was in full operational service when the war began. It wasn't until 1944 that its replacement, the Curtiss SB2C, was finally ready, but this monstrous truck was full of bugs and chronic ills. SBD men embraced their mount with fanaticism, and well they might. Most of the Japanese fleet and naval air forces had been destroyed. For three crucial years of concentrated air war the Dauntless carried the flag. Some called her the Barge, the Clunk, or the Daunty Lass. To malign the SBD, in retrospect, is punishable by a full round of drinks or even a stint in the Foreign Legion. Truly, this mighty marvel wrote most of the history of the air war in the Pacific.[83]

THE *YORKTOWN* HYDRA

With the newly constructed USS *Essex* (CV-9) joining the Pacific fleet in May 1943, the United States industrial might started impacting the balance of the war. The second of twenty-four *Essex*-class carriers was originally to be named the *Bonhomme Richard* in honor of John Paul Jones's flagship during the American Revolution, but after the loss of the first *Yorktown* (CV-5) at Midway, she was rechristened *Yorktown* (CV-10). The existence of two carriers both named *Yorktown* caused some confusion, particularly to the Japanese who believed that they had sunk

---

83   This is the wonderful description of the SBD Dauntless Dive Bomber on the Planes in Action Calendar issued by Bob Gibson's Desert Life—a senior living facility owned by Bob near Tucson, Arizona—in the 1980s. Although the author is not specifically known, it surely smacks of Hoot's pen. A nationally distributed calendar by the United States Air Force Museum for 1981 also featured the exploits of a handful of American combat pilots during the war, including those of Hoot.

Yorktown once at Coral Sea and twice at Midway. So, she emerged in a newer and bigger form only months after she submerged at Midway. To the Japanese, the *Yorktown* must have seemed like the mythical Hydra, which grew two new heads whenever one was decapitated.[84]

· ❧ ·

THE BIG E

When the keel of the *USS Enterprise* CV-6 was laid on July 16, 1934, she had a full load displacement of 32,000 tons. She was the seventh US fighting ship to bear the name of a perpetual symbol in the great struggle to retain American liberty, justice, and freedom since the initial days of the Revolutionary War. The *Enterprise* was built by the Newport News Shipbuilding and Drydock Company of Virginia and launched on October 3, 1936, under the sponsorship of Mrs. Claude A. Swanson, wife of the Secretary of the Navy. As the new carrier slid down the ways, Mrs. Swanson quoted a line from Shakespeare's *Othello* that would gain increasing significance in the years to follow:

"May she also say, with just pride—I have done my state some service."

Mrs. Claude A. Swanson, wife of the Secretary of the Navy, christens the USS *Enterprise* (CV-6) on October 3, 1936, at Newport News, Virginia. (US Navy)

---

84   Symonds, *The Battle of Midway*, 360.

She would become the first carrier to be awarded the Presidential Unit Citation and also win the Navy Unit Commendation. No other aircraft carrier received both of these recognitions for service during World War II. The Big E also carried twenty battle stars. Of the more than twenty major actions of the Pacific War, *Enterprise* engaged in all but two. Her planes and guns downed 911 enemy planes. Her bombers sank 71 ships, and damaged or destroyed 192 more. Her presence inspired pride in the Allies and sparked fear in the hearts of the enemy.

Enterprise was decommissioned on February 17, 1947, and stricken from the List of Naval Vessels on Oct. 2, 1956.

This was the greatest achievement of all the achievements of the war, and I think also of all the events known to us in history, the most decisive for the victor, the most ruinous for the conquered. They were utterly defeated at all points and endured no small sufferings, to no end.

—Thucydides: *Peloponnesian War*, Book VII

EPILOGUE

Bob Gibson, 1946

AT THE END of 1942, Hoot was one of a small band of carrier pilots left on the only carrier remaining in the Pacific fight. He had over 600 combat flight hours, fought in three of the five carrier battles of the war, and had been in thirteen named battles of the war, including Guadalcanal and Borneo, the first and last amphibious landings of WWII. Hoot killed thousands of Japanese soldiers, and so he had a $200,000 price on his head, put there by the Japanese. It was a time when "So much was owed by so many to so few." That generation of young warriors has passed but their courage and sacrifice will, we trust, live on.

After the war, Hoot did not stay in the US Navy or ever fly an airplane again, and never returned to teaching music or band, although he did conduct the Tucson Symphony on one occasion. He became a stockbroker, worked for Marshall Field Enterprises, sold house trailers, manufactured quartz crystals for electronics, sold real estate, and was an entrepreneur, usually a decade ahead of his time on most projects. He recognized the need for geriatric care with America's growing number of aging citizens and developed a hundred acres in Tucson, Arizona, where the Northwest Hospital, Desert Life Nursing Home, and many physicians' offices are now located. He made and lost fortunes over his lifetime but never felt he had had a bad day after his rare personal survival in the Pacific War. He'd whistle while driving his car to the creditor to be repossessed rather than them having to come get it. In good times, he gave millions to the Tucson Symphony and to the Metropolitan Opera.

Bob was part of America's longest continuous poker game—over forty years—at the Mountain Oyster Club in Tucson. He was a proud member of the *Military Order of the Carabao* and attended most of their Annual Wallows at the Army Navy Club in Washington with his World War II buddies. Bob married two gorgeous women, though not at the same time, and raised three sons. He died in Tucson in 2002 at age eighty-three. He has a headstone near his family's large memorial at the cemetery in Unionville, Missouri. Although the Gibson family monument is proudly inscribed with the description, *Average Americans*, he was far, far from it, as you also know now.

ACKNOWLEDGMENTS

UNCLE BOB'S YOUNGER sister was my mom, Millie. She had the same dive-bomber courage and acute mentality as her brother. She dove into life. Her great stories about Unionville and the Gibson clan were instilled in the hearts and minds of my family early on. Reading the books on Bob's exploits whetted our appetite for adventure and the drive to tell a good story.

Bob's memoirs were a good story on their own, though. That he shared his memories with his sons and nephews makes them that much more special. One weekend in the mid-1990s, Bob invited all his sons and nephews to Tucson for our own *Wallow* so that he could tell the story of his Pacific War journey while he still could. For many hours and many cigars and drinks over two days as well as dinners at the vaunted Mountain Oyster Club, Bob became Hoot again and gave us the skinny on his war . . . and the Royal Hawaiian battles. I knew then that it was too good not to retell.

My attempt to do just that was made easy by having his wonderful memoirs and the materials and papers collected by my Grandmother Gibson from the war. It also was greatly assisted by the many Pacific War Navy historians and others who covered the fight with their own books, including Eugene Burns, Eric Hammel, and Stephen Moore, the first to work Bob's memoirs into his compelling *Hell's Island*, which of course gave me the title idea. Other scholars and writers on Hoot's part of WWII in the Pacific are Stanley Johnson, Richard Frank, Ian Toll, James Hornfischer, Jeffrey Cox, and others listed in the sources below. Their inspiring stories and details of the battles in the Pacific added texture and context to Bob's recollections, and for that I am most grateful.

My main acknowledgments for this story go to those who fought in it, Bob's close friends Dave Chaffey, Steve Czarnecki, Dick Jaccard, Ralph Goddard, and many others who did not survive the war—and the few carrier pilots who did, like Bud Lucier, Rod Hoogerswerf, and Hal Buell, whom I met and introduced for a speech when Hal was in his nineties. These SBD dive bombers were the heart and soul of America's first line of defense in the Pacific war. With great honor, appreciation, and grateful acknowledgment, this is their story, too.

BIBLIOGRAPHY

Brand, Max. *Fighter Squadron at Guadalcanal.* Annapolis: Naval Institute Press, 1996.

Buell, Harold L. *Dauntless Helldivers: A Dive-Bomber Pilot's Epic Story of the Carrier Battles.* New York: Orion, 1991.

Burns, Eugene. *Then There Was One: The USS. Enterprise and the First Year of the War.* New York: Harcourt, Brace, 1944.

Clemens, Martin. *Alone on Guadalcanal: A Coastwatcher's Story.* Annapolis: Naval Institute Press, 1998.

Coombe, Jack D. *Derailing the Tokyo Express: The Naval Battles for the Solomon Islands That Sealed Japan's Fate.* Harrisburg, Pa.: Stackpole, 1991.

Costello, John. *The Pacific War.* New York: William Morrow, 1982.

Cox, Jeffrey R. *Morning Star, Midnight Sun: The Early Guadalcanal-Solomons Campaign of World War II, August—October 1942.* Oxford: Osprey, 2018.

_____. *Blazing Star, Setting Sun: The Guadalcanal-Solomons Campaign, November 1942—March 1943*. Oxford: Osprey, 2020.

Ewing, Steve. *USS Enterprise (CV-6): The Most Decorated Ship of World War II*. Missoula, Mont.: Pictorial Histories Publishing Company, 1996.

Frank, Richard B. *Guadalcanal: The Definitive Account of the Landmark Battle*. New York: Random House, 1990.

Gibson, Robert D. *Average American at Guadalcanal*. Unpublished manuscript, 2002.

Gibson, Robert D. *Slow But Deadly. A Navy Dive Bomber Pilot Makes a Pact with the Moon. A True Adventure Story*. Unpublished memoir, 1998. *Personal Papers of Robert D. Gibson*, author's possession.

Gibson, Lt. Cdr. Robert D., USNR (Ret.). Interview with William J. Shinneman, 10 July 1993 transcript, the Oral History Archive, American Airpower Heritage Museum, Midland, Texas, 6-7.

Hammel, Eric. *Carrier Clash: The Invasion of Guadalcanal & the Battle of the Eastern Solomons*. Pacifica, Calif.: Pacifica Press, 1997.

_____. *Carrier Strike: The Battle of the Santa Cruz Islands*. Pacifica, Calif.: Pacifica Press, 1999.

_____. *Guadalcanal, The Carrier Battles: The Pivotal Aircraft Carrier Battles of the Eastern Solomons and Santa Cruz*. New York: Crown,1987.

_____. *Guadalcanal: Decision at Sea: The Naval Battle of Guadalcanal, November 13-15, 1942*. New York: Crown, 1988.

Hornfischer, James D. *Neptune's Inferno: The US Navy at Guadalcanal.* New York: Bantam, 2011.

Johnston, Stanley. *The Grim Reapers.* New York: E.P. Dutton, 1943.

Keeney, L. Douglas and William S. Butler. *This is Guadalcanal: The Original Combat Photography.* New York: William Morrow, 1998.

Lundstrom, John B. *The First Team: Pacific Naval Air Combat from Pearl Harbor to Midway.* Annapolis: Naval Institute Press, 1984.

_____. *The First Team and the Guadalcanal Campaign: Naval Fighter Combat from August to November 1942.* Annapolis: Naval Institute Press, 1994.

_____. *Black Shoe Carrier Admiral: Frank Jack Fletcher at Coral Sea, Midway, and Guadalcanal.* Annapolis: Naval Institute Press, 2006.

Manchester, William. *Goodbye, Darkness: A Memoir of the Pacific War.* Boston: Little Brown, 1979.

Mears, Lieutenant Frederick. *Carrier Combat: Battle Action with an American Torpedo Plane Pilot.* Garden City, N.Y.: Doubleday, Doran, 1944.

Moore, Stephen L. *The Battle for Hell's Island: How a Small Band of Carrier Dive-Bombers Helped Save Guadalcanal.* New York: NAL Caliber/Penguin Random, 2015.

_____. *Pacific.Payback: The Carrier Aviators Who Avenged Pearl Harbor at the Battle of Midway.* New York: NAL Caliber/Penguin Random, 2014.

Morison, Samuel Eliot, *History of the United States Naval Operations in World War II, Volume III: The Rising Sun in the Pacific, 1931 - April 1942*. Boston: Little, Brown, 1948.

_____. *History of the United States Naval Operations in World War II, Volume IV: Coral Sea, Midway and Submarine Actions, May 1942-August 1942*. Boston: Little, Brown, 1949.

_____. *History of the United States Naval Operations in World War II, Volume V: The Struggle for Guadalcanal, August 1942 – February 1943*. Boston: Little, Brown, 1949.

_____. *History of the United States Naval Operations in World War II, Volume XIII: The Liberation of the Philippines: Luzon, Mindanao, the Visyas, 1944-1945*. Boston: Little, Brown, 1959.

_____. *The Two-Ocean War*. Boston: Little, Brown, 1963.

O'Donnell, Patrick K. *Into the Rising Sun: In their Own Words, World War II's Pacific Veterans Reveal the Heart of Combat*. New York: Free Press, 2002.

Smith, William Ward. *Midway, Turning Point of the Pacific*. New York: Thomas Y. Crowell, 1966.

Stafford, Commander Edward P. *The Big E: The Story of the USS Enterprise*. Annapolis: Naval Institute Press, 1962.

Symonds, Craig L. *The Battle of Midway*. New York: Oxford University Press, 2011.

Tillman, Barrett. *Enterprise, America's Fightingest Ship and The Men Who Helped Win World War II*. New York: Simon Schuster, 2012.

_____. *The Dauntless Dive Bomber of World War Two.* Annapolis: Naval Institute Press, 1976.

Toland, John. *The Rising Sun: The Decline and Fall of the Japanese Empire, 1936-1945.* Two Volumes. New York: Random House, 1970.

Toll, Ian W. *Pacific Crucible: War at Sea in the Pacific, 1941-1942.* New York: Norton, 2012.

_____. *The Conquering Tide: War in the Pacific Islands, 1942-1944.* New York: Norton, 2015.

_____. *Twilight of the Gods: War in the Western Pacific, 1944-1945.* New York: Norton, 2020.

Twinning, Merrill B., Lieutenant General USMC (Ret.). *No Bended Knee: The Battle for Guadalcanal.* New York: Presidio, 1996.

Weinberg, Gerhard L. *World in the Balance: Behind the Scenes of World War II.* University Press of New England, Hanover, N.H., 1981

Wheelan, Joseph. *Midnight in the Pacific: Guadalcanal, The World War Battle that Turned the Tide of the War.* Boston: Da Capo Press, 2017.

ABOUT THE AUTHOR

Kirk Gibson Warner retired as an Army colonel after thirty-three years of military service. He is the author of *Zone of Action: A JAG's Journey Inside Operations Cobra II and Iraqi Freedom*. He was a featured "hero" on CNN's *Lou Dobbs' Tonight* for his service in Iraq. He served as deputy legal counsel to three chairmen of the Joint Chiefs of Staff and commanded units from company to brigade levels. He is a graduate of the Army War College and has five graduate degrees. Kirk is a partner and senior trial lawyer with Raleigh's largest law firm, Smith Anderson.

Kirk and his wife Diane live in Wrightsville Beach, North Carolina, with their dog, Wally. Like his uncle Bob Gibson, Kirk is a member of the *Military Order of the Carabao* and enjoys a good wallow. He is also an avid historian and lifelong fan of his uncle Hoot—an outstanding and undeniably true American hero.

www.ingramcontent.com/pod-product-compliance
Lightning Source LLC
Chambersburg PA
CBHW031938090426
42811CB00002B/222